F. 28.

F.16'.

F.17

F.12.

F. 21.

F. 22

MÉGATHERIUM.

20.

Charles Darwin

Charles Darwin

John Chancellor

Taplinger Publishing Company
New York

First published in the United States in 1976 by
Taplinger Publishing Co., Inc.
New York, New York

Library of Congress Catalog Card Number: 76–5175
ISBN 0–8008–1434–7

Contents

Introduction

WITH MOST GREAT MEN AND WOMEN it is possible to argue about the extent of their influence. The life of Charles Darwin poses no such question. His discovery of 'Evolution' – to telescope an intricate subject into one word – cannot be overrated. Nor was it underestimated by his contemporaries. As John Chancellor shows, that little green book, *The Origin of Species*, shook both Victorian science and religion. They were never the same again.

Darwin was comparable in the nineteenth century only with Marx and Freud, each of whom dropped his bombs on the old superstructures of economics and psychology respectively. Countless studies have been made of all three with scarcely a thought to their private lives. There is nothing wrong in this. You can understand *Das Kapital* without realizing that Marx worked in the British Museum. Similarly, you can grasp Darwin's theory of how new species developed on this earth, without knowing that he had a charming wife called Emma Wedgwood and ten children. John Chancellor, however, sets out deliberately to balance Darwin's public discoveries with his personal life. And what a saga it is.

The winds of 'Evolution' had fanned the imagination of Charles's grandfather, Erasmus, long before they blew a gale in his grandson's mind. Again, Charles's poor educational record is a classic example of mysterious talents unable to fit into ordinary categories. Then comes the incomparable voyage of the *Beagle*, with Darwin's discovery of fossils on the Galapagos Islands, which he himself called 'the origin of all my views'. The origin, so to speak, of *The Origin*. Lastly, the dramatic publication of the book, with all the consequences and controversies which ensued. The ancient and rancorous line-up of opinion behind either 'apes' or 'angels' as man's predecessors is put by John Chancellor into proper perspective. Though a religious believer, he is scrupulously fair to those who hold that Darwin rightly threw away the baby with the bathwater. In other words, that he threw away the Creator, along with a ludicrous theory of creation advanced by some contemporary philosophers. These so-called 'Catastrophists' envisaged

7

a God who every so often decreed a universally destructive flood or earthquake, after which He would obligingly re-create the species of living creatures from scratch.

As a problematic thread running through Darwin's whole life is the question of his neurotic invalidism. John Chancellor refuses to be drawn into the dangerous delights of retrospective diagnosis. But he gives a fascinating account of the many theories which have nevertheless been offered by others.

A man as simple, patient, gentle and good as Darwin yet scourged with disease, whether mental or physical – how, one asks, did the flame of inspiration come to seize upon and inhabit that particular brain and body? The answer must surely be in terms of his own immortal theory. It was not Darwin's business to explain *why* certain species adapted themselves to their opportunities better than others. He simply saw that they made the transmutation. Somehow Darwin himself was transmuted from a semi-educated devotee of partridge-shooting to one of the world's geniuses. We can only read and wonder.

Elizabeth Longford

Importance of Erasmus

CHARLES
DARWIN

The ORIGIN of SPECIES

On 24 NOVEMBER 1859 *The Origin of Species* was published. The author was Charles Darwin, an invalid naturalist who lived a secluded life in the country with his large family. The success of his book and the howls of horror which greeted it surprised this diffident man who had told his publisher, John Murray, that the proposed printing of 1,250 copies was 'too large an edition'. In fact, it sold out within a few hours and, from that day to this, there has been an uninterrupted flow of new editions and commentaries on the book.

The Origin of Species was the most important book of the nineteenth century. Its achievement was to teach people to believe in evolution. Not only the general public but also many naturalists were horrified by the theories, or by the implications of the theories, which Darwin propounded. He was, they said, trying to dethrone man from his proper place in the scheme of things and to challenge the incontrovertible truths of the Bible. He had dared to question the view that the human race was a unique and lofty species, created by God in His own image and quite independent of every other form of living thing. He suggested instead that species – that is, plants and animals and other living organisms, including man – had started as quite different creatures from those we see today: that they had undergone all sorts of subtle changes over the years, thus giving rise, by slow and natural processes, to new species.

The press lost no time in dismissing Darwin's researches into the mutability of species as the 'ape theory', because of the idea that man was descended from the ape. He became the bogeyman of the godfearing Victorian middle classes. Disraeli sensed their fears and made his famous remark about being on the side of the angels.

Darwin's exemplary life and the infinite patience and thoroughness with which he tested his theories made him all the more feared. In the eighteenth century it was common for public figures to be lampooned as animals; the idea was funny and far-fetched. Darwin showed that it was not quite so funny, that there was not all that much difference between man and other animals. The close and powerful reasoning and the detailed evidence which characterize his book forced the world to take it seriously.

Today people do not tell their children with bated breath that Darwin had said we were monkeys rather than angels. His ideas on the evolution of living things are considered so obvious as to be almost trite. We are 'Darwinists' even if we do not know it. He lingers in our minds as an earnest, hard-working Victorian naturalist

PREVIOUS PAGES Erasmus Darwin *(right)* indulging in one of his favourite pastimes – a game of chess – with his son Erasmus.

OPPOSITE Charles Darwin at the time of the publication of *The Origin of Species*.

OPPOSITE Mrs Elizabeth Pole who became the second wife of Erasmus Darwin, painted by Joseph Wright of Derby. The portrait is now at Down House.

LEFT Breadsall Priory, the home of Dr and Mrs Erasmus Darwin in Derby.

BELOW Wright's portrait of Erasmus.

of impeccable morality and of disinterested attachment to scientific truth. Although biologists no longer bother to read his works, Darwin is remembered by those who take an interest in the history of thought. Why otherwise should copies of the first edition of *The Origin of Species* fetch nearly £1,000? This dull-looking little book in dark green cloth is not even relieved by pictures!

That this illustrious Englishman should have suffered from neglect is strange. First of all, there is something wholesome and refreshing in the very Englishness of his personality. His tastes were simple and unaffected; in his youth he liked the robust, open-air life – riding to hounds and partridge shooting; he loved the country and hated cities; he fitted quite naturally into his family's comfortable middle-class life in the west Midlands and he was not ashamed of the fact that their money had been earned rather than inherited; he disliked humbug and hypocrisy and had no wish, once he had been on his interesting journey around the world, ever to go abroad again or to learn a foreign language.

This reassuring 'Englishness' was shaken by a sudden and dramatic awareness of the mysteries of Nature. Darwin became obsessed with the desire to find the key to the secret of living things. He became what is known as a 'paranoiac thinker', unable for the rest of his life to stop brooding and writing about the great theory which he thought he had discovered. He appears, through a deliberate effort of the will, to have turned himself into an old man before he was thirty. For the next forty years, there is nothing more to say about him; he wrote and rested in his happy family home, where he died aged seventy-three.

Was evolution in the air in the middle of the last century and was Darwin's cogently written little book merely a summary of what intelligent people were already thinking? Darwin himself was not of this opinion: 'It has sometimes been said that the success of the "Origin" proved that "the subject was in the air" or "that men's minds were prepared for it". I do not think that this is strictly true, for I occasionally sounded not a few naturalists, and never happened to come across a single one who seemed to doubt about the permanence of species.' Darwin may, in his isolation, have believed this, but it does not appear, from the literature of the period, to be strictly true. Whenever two or more naturalists were gathered together, questions such as 'What is a species?' or 'How did species begin?' invariably cropped up, and Darwin's book provided for many the answers for which they had been groping.

OPPOSITE Erasmus Darwin, 'British physician and poet' – an engraving after the painting by Rawlinson.

16

It is true that many scientists were frightened of the possible consequences of Darwin's theories, even when they found them scientifically convincing. They feared that they might encourage notions of a brutal, mechanical universe, with no allowance being made for the moral and metaphysical parts of Nature. Events have shown that they were right to have such fears. Darwin, although a gentleman and an amateur, had the blinkered, insensitive approach to his work of the modern business tycoon or scientist. He was unable to appreciate the important differences between man and other animals or to understand that the evolution of human beings from a savage to a civilized state was more a cultural than a biological change. He had no sense of history and dismissed with truculent impatience suggestions that he owed any intellectual debts to thinkers of the past, even to his remarkable grandfather, Erasmus Darwin.

It is interesting that Darwin should have been adopted by the godless materialistic movements of our own day. Karl Marx had asked whether he might dedicate *Das Kapital* to the author of *The Origin of Species*. Darwin refused, not because he particularly objected to its contents, but because he thought that its anti-religious views might cause 'concern' to certain members of his family! In this respect Darwin was the inheritor of the eighteenth-century scientific and utilitarian attitudes of his two grandfathers.

Some time between 1759 and 1764 a meeting took place between two unusual men – Erasmus Darwin and Josiah Wedgwood. They immediately became friends and remained so for the next thirty years. Neither lived to learn of the birth of their joint grandson, Charles Darwin. In their thoughts and actions, both left their mark on the social and scientific changes of their day, and may claim to have shaped considerably the personality of their illustrious grandson.

The Darwin lineage is neither ancient nor distinguished. Their family records cannot be traced further back than the middle of the sixteenth century. Mention is made in 1542 of two Darwins, father and son, both named William. They were yeomen of Marton, near Gainsborough, in Lincolnshire, and their surname is thought to have been taken from one of the various rivers Derwent which are found in the north country. Although the name is now unusual in England, it was fairly common in the neighbourhood of Sheffield in Lancashire in the old days, where it was spelled in a variety of ways – Darwen, Darwynne, Derwent, etc. The genera-

OPPOSITE Josiah Wedgwood, founder of the Etruria potteries and maternal grandfather of Charles Darwin, in an engraving from the portrait by Sir Joshua Reynolds.

19

tions went by and slowly the Darwins, by prudent marriages and their own merits, climbed the social ladder. During the reign of Charles I they had begun to be of a certain consequence. William Darwin the fifth (1620-75) had inherited from his father a prosperous and enlarged estate at Marton, which he very nearly lost after the Civil War – the result of fighting for the King as Captain-Lieutenant in Sir William Pelham's troop of horse. Instead, he was fined heavily. After the Restoration he was made Recorder of Lincoln, having practised as a barrister at Lincoln's Inn during the Commonwealth, during which time he probably met and married his wife, the daughter of Erasmus Earle, sergeant-at-law, from whom his great-grandson Erasmus derived his Christian name. The station of the Darwins was yet further improved by the marriage of the Recorder's son, another William, to the heiress of Robert Waring, who belonged to a good Staffordshire family. She inherited the manse and hall of Elston near Newark, a handsome Elizabethan house, which became in due course the property of William's son Robert, the father of Erasmus Darwin. In Robert Darwin, the great-grandfather of Charles, we begin to perceive certain family traits. He was modest, dignified and sombre, a temperance advocate and with a pronounced taste for natural history. His eldest son, Robert, who inherited Elston and died there a bachelor at ninety-two, wrote *Principia Botanica: or A Concise and Easy Introduction to the General Botany of Linnaeus*. It ran into several editions and was later commended by Charles Darwin as containing 'many curious notes on biology – a subject wholly neglected in England in the last century'.

Erasmus Darwin, the younger brother of the bachelor-botanist, remains to this day the most genial, ebullient and idiosyncratic of all the Darwins. He was born at Elston Hall on 12 December 1731. The multiplicity of interests which characterized his life may be listed roughly as the exact sciences, animal and plant biology, technology and poetry. His later reputation has suffered from his very versatility; his ingenious comical experiments and his, in the words of his grandson, 'overpowering tendency to theorize and generalize', without testing his theories to any great extent, explain the summary treatment he is given in books on eighteenth-century science and thought. Coleridge coined the word 'Darwinizing' as a contemptuous reference to what he regarded as Erasmus's habit of indulging in wild speculation. It is, however, more likely that Coleridge was alarmed by the evolutionary views which were developed in Erasmus's writings, particularly in

Zoonomia, and that he was, with his remarkable insight, anticipating the religious objections of the Victorians to *The Origin of
Species*. Many distinguished thinkers and men of science in
eighteenth-century England managed to combine scientific ardour
with religious certainty. In France, on the other hand, most, if not
all, respected thinkers were militant enemies of religion, and it was
even difficult to find in the Church itself an intelligent prelate who
would admit to believing the Christian mysteries. In that most
Christian and Catholic country, scepticism, atheism and agnosti-
cism carried all before them. Things were not quite so bad in England and what was known as the holy alliance between science and
religion continued until the end of the century.

Erasmus Darwin, although not a sceptic like the French
'philosophes', was scornful of organized religion and he included
such Christian notions as fear of Hell in his medical catalogue of
diseases. Coleridge, who thought Erasmus had 'a greater range of
knowledge than any other man in Europe', considered his lack of
interest in religion to be his greatest intellectual shortcoming: 'He
thinks in a *new* train on all subjects except on religion.' Erasmus,
in his *Zoonomia*, a medical textbook which contained the essentials of his evolutionary thinking, speaks of the 'Great First Cause'
with apparent conviction, but recommends as a cure for Christian
credulity that we 'increase our knowledge of the laws of nature'.
In England at that time, when the most admired and powerful
minds were grappling with the problem of reconciling Christian
dogmas to new scientific and philosophical ideas, Erasmus's
rejection of Christianity was considered to be superficial and
eccentric. A century later this would not have been the case.

This judgment of Coleridge and others has been damaging to
Erasmus's reputation. In fact, his belief in the beneficent results
of the study of nature was the basis of eighteenth-century
Christianity. 'Nature' had replaced revelation as the basis of
religion. The new scientific movement, as illustrated by the works
of Galileo, Bacon, Descartes and Newton, had discredited supernatural explanations of the physical world. It was not, however,
anti-religious. The great scientists all believed that they were
serving the cause of religion as well as of science. Bacon had said
that the study of science was the study of the *works* of God. No one
doubted that the findings of science would go hand in hand with
Christian presuppositions and everyone, scientist and churchman
alike, could rejoice with Pope that 'Nature and Nature's laws
lay hid in night; God said, *Let Newton be!* and all was light!' If

22   The birthplace of Erasmus Darwin, Elston Hall as it was before 1754.

Erasmus did not quite see things in this way, although he very nearly did, the reason may have been not that he lacked intellectual and spiritual depth, but because he thought about the biological ancestry of man, and biology was, as his grandson later said, a subject wholly neglected in England in the last century.

This, then, is a brief sketch of the religious and scientific 'climate of opinion' in Erasmus's day. We have very little information about his early life. He spent nine happy years at Chesterfield School where he gained the reputation of a wag and a wit of a rather pedantic sort. Then in 1750, he went up, with his two elder brothers, to St John's, Cambridge, where he read classics, mathematics and medicine, and wrote poems, one of which, on the death of Frederick, Prince of Wales, was later published in the *European Magazine* for 1795. In 1754 he went to Edinburgh to study medicine where he is quoted as 'sacrificing to both Bacchus and Venus', but he soon discovered that he could not continue his devotion to both deities without destroying his health and constitution. 'He therefore resolved to relinquish Bacchus, but his affection for Venus was retained to the last period of his life.' After taking his MD at Cambridge, Erasmus decided to set up in practice at Nottingham as a doctor.

For various reasons Nottingham was a failure. Erasmus failed to get many patients and he amused himself instead by learning shorthand, writing letters in Latin and versifying. After a couple of months he moved to Lichfield, the cathedral city of Staffordshire and the home town of David Garrick and Dr Johnson. He had a letter of introduction to Canon Seward, whose house was the literary centre of Lichfield and whose daughter Anna was later to write an entertaining book about his life in Lichfield, *Memoirs of the life of Dr Darwin, chiefly during his residence at Lichfield, with anecdotes of his friends and criticisms of his writings.* Erasmus got off to a good start by bringing a dying young gentleman 'of family, future and consequence' back to life by applying a novel course of treatment after all the most celebrated local doctors had pronounced the case to be hopeless. This established him as Lichfield's leading physician and his practice increased quickly to £1,000 a year.

As Erasmus's appearance was one of the unforgettable, if not particularly attractive things about him, becoming with the years steadily more grotesque, we should let Anna Seward describe it in her own words, when he arrived at Lichfield in 1756 aged twenty-four:

He was somewhat above the middle size, his form athletic, and inclined to corpulence; his limbs too heavy for exact proportion. The traces of a severe smallpox; features and countenance, which when they were not animated by social pleasures, were rather saturnine than sprightly; a stoop in the shoulders, and the then professional appendage, a large full-bottomed wig, gave, at that early period of life, an appearance of nearly twice the years he bore. Florid health, and the earnest of good humour, a sunny smile, on entering a room, and on first accosting his friends, rendered in his youth, that exterior agreeable, to which beauty and symmetry had not been propitious.

Erasmus had an extreme stammer; he was conscious of his superiority to the general standard of intellect and he avenged argument in conversation with savage sarcasm and wounding irony. He 'avowed a conviction of the pernicious effects of all vinous fluids on the youthful and healthy constitution'. If he drank a glass or two of English wine, he mixed it with water. He despised foreign wines: 'If you must drink wine, he said, let it be home made.' His influence and example were claimed by Miss Seward to have sobered the county of Derby.

A very attractive aspect of him was his generosity; he never took fees from poor patients, whom he supplied with food, money and advice. 'Generosity, wit, and science, were his household gods.' Miss Seward ends her sketch by telling us of the final present which Nature had bestowed upon his mind, 'the seducing and often dangerous gift of a highly poetic imagination'. These gifts he repressed for thirty years for fear they might harm his reputation as a doctor. 'With the wisdom of Ulysses, he bound himself to the medical mast, that he might not follow those delusive sirens, the muses, or be considered their avowed votary.'

Soon after arriving in Lichfield, he married Mary Howard, the seventeen-year-old daughter of a neighbour of the Sewards. She appeared to possess every virtue – beauty, a strong intellect, gaiety and sweetness. 'But, alas, upon her early youth, and a too delicate constitution, the frequency of her maternal situation, had probably a baneful effect.' She had five children in nine years and was an invalid for several years before she died in 1770, after thirteen years of marriage. Their children were all born in an old half-timbered house near the Cathedral. The house was separated from the street by a deep, narrow dell. Erasmus cleared it, made a terrace along the bank and planted the slope with lilac and rose bushes. It was in this *rus in urbe* that Erasmus entertained his many friends. The social position of doctors has always been equivocal; in Lichfield in those days they were admitted to dances but not to card-assemblies and, when calling at country houses, were received in the housekeeper's quarters rather than in the drawing-room. Erasmus was not bound by such conventions, and to the respect in which he was held by all classes was added pride that he should have preferred to remain in Lichfield rather than to accept King George III's invitation to come to London as his personal physician.

It was at about this time, as we have seen, that Erasmus met Josiah Wedgwood. A delightful and enduring friendship was about to start. It is quite likely that Wedgwood first came to Erasmus as a patient, although his house at Burslem was about thirty miles from Lichfield. He had been enfeebled by a virulent attack of smallpox when a boy, and this had particularly affected his right knee. Later he was to have his leg amputated.

The Wedgwood ancestry was similar to that of the Darwins — yeomen slowly rising to the status of small landowners. They were, however, so prolific that, despite the possession of landed property, the younger sons were sometimes obliged to earn a living in the local industry. Hence Josiah's father and various uncles and cousins became potters – some masters, some journey-men. Josiah was a boy when his father died and he then started work in the pottery of his eldest brother at Burslem, where he soon became an expert 'thrower' on the wheel. The weakness in his knee returned and he was forced to abandon the thrower's bench and occupy himself in other departments of the potter's art.

His steady rise to fame and riches now started. As everyone knows, Josiah Wedgwood became the greatest potter of his age, his work always marked by reticence in form and colour, com-bining, whenever possible, beauty and utility and reflecting the refinement and serenity of his own mind and character. When he first met Erasmus, he was planning a new factory between Burslem and Stoke-on-Trent. Erasmus suggested for it the name 'Etruria' because he thought that Josiah had rediscovered some special enamelling process known only to the Etruscans. Erasmus designed a horizontal windmill for grinding colours and mixing clay. It was erected at the Etruria works and remained in use for many years. Erasmus was of considerable help to Josiah in furthering the realization of his cherished project – the extension of the canal system to Etruria. This resulted in the opening of the Trent and Mersey Canal (the 'Grand Trunk Canal') in 1777, which passed through the Etruria estate.

Etruria Hall, home of the
Wedgwoods, named at the
suggestion of Erasmus
Darwin.

Most of Erasmus's friends at this time were members of the famous Lunar Society. They held monthly or 'lunar' meetings at each other's houses near the time of the full moon, so that they might ride home by moonlight. The society flourished in the 1770s; there were about a dozen members and each could bring a guest. Josiah Wedgwood was not himself a 'lunatic', as Erasmus called the members, but he was a frequent guest. There were some distinguished names among the 'lunatics' and their guests – James Watt, of steam-engine fame, Richard Lovell Edgeworth, the father of Maria Edgeworth, John Baskerville, the printer, and Joseph Priestley, the great scientist and apostle of modern Unitarianism, who represented all that was best in the mind and spirit of the late eighteenth century.

The 'lunatics' all believed in progress and perfectibility: hence the buoyant atmosphere of their discussions which were not, unfortunately, recorded. They revolved largely around the latest developments in science and technology, and Erasmus no doubt diverted members with accounts of his latest inventions, such as a talking-machine, a carriage which was resistant to overturning and dozens of other mechanical devices. The 'lunatics' and their friends shared the same attitude to life. They were fascinated by science and invention; they were followers of Rousseau, whom Erasmus once met reclining in a cave near Lichfield; they were radical in their politics, welcoming both the American War of Independence and the French Revolution; their religious views were rational and 'heretical', although nominally Christian. They all, no doubt, believed that a dawn, in which it would be bliss to be alive, was about to break upon their generation.

After his wife's death in 1770, Erasmus consoled himself by taking a mistress whose name was Parker and who bore him two daughters. He also turned to botany and to verse and to the companionship of his biographer Anna Seward. He founded the Lichfield Botanic Society, which had two members other than himself, and he laid out a botanical garden on the outskirts of Lichfield. He turned a brook into small lakes and adorned their borders with different classes of plants, thus, in Anna Seward's words, 'uniting the Linnean science with the charm of landscape'.

In 1781 Erasmus married again – the widow of Colonel Sacheverel Pole of Radbourne Hall near Derby. He had been in love with her for some time and had addressed to her many passionate poems before her husband's death in 1780. Many were no doubt written during the long hours he spent on his rounds as he bumped along

OPPOSITE Jean-Jacques Rousseau, seen here in an etching by Naudet.

31

the country roads in his chaise. An early biographer of Josiah Wedgwood has suggested that the jerky movements of a chaise explained why he expressed his thoughts and feelings through verse rather than prose, which 'required a concentration of thought incompatible with constant movement and professional interruptions'.

Erasmus's success in winning the hand of a rich and attractive young widow illustrates the triumph of intellect and character over other disabilities. Although not yet fifty, he had not worn well; he was so fat that a hole had to be cut in the table to accommodate him at meals; his teeth had fallen out and his mouth, when he spoke, disclosed the ravages of time. Nevertheless, it was a very happy marriage and his second wife bore him seven children.

It was during his years in and near Derby that Erasmus wrote his books and poems, so popular in their time but more or less unreadable today. The first of these strange and brilliant works was *The Botanic Garden*, which was divided into two parts, *The Economy of Vegetation* and *The Loves of the Plants*. Erasmus's purpose was, in the words of his preface, 'to inlist imagination under the banner of science' and to recommend to the reader's attention 'the immortal works of the celebrated Swedish Naturalist Linneus'. At the end of the eighteenth century, no book could fail to be a best-seller if it contained the name of Linnaeus, that industrious Swede who reclassified the plant kingdom by introducing binomial nomenclature, that is by giving every plant a specific as well as a generic name. This appears today to be a fairly pedestrian achievement, but not so in the eighteenth century. Rousseau said that his *Philosophia Botanica*, one of Linnaeus's little books on plant classification, 'had more wisdom in it than the biggest of folios'. The English appropriated Linnaeus as they had appropriated Handel; every English child was taught to revere the name of Linnaeus who, like Newton in the physical sciences, had brought order out of chaos and revealed the clarity and symmetry of God's works in the biological sphere. Small wonder, then, that *The Botanic Garden* ran into many editions. Erasmus was paid £1,000 for each of the sections. Both poems read like a pot-pourri of Erasmus's miscellaneous interests, expressed in pedantic and painlessly composed heroic couplets. 'Pompous rhyme', said Lord Byron, 'The scenery is its sole recommendation.' Anna Seward, on the other hand, thought it 'one of the richest effusions of the poetic mind that has shed lustre over Europe in the eighteenth century'.

A silhouette of Mrs Pole.

After *The Botanic Garden* came *Zoonomia, or The Laws of Organic Life*, published in 1794 and 1796. In this remarkable two-volume work, Erasmus put forward very explicit evolutionary views. These are, however, submerged by the book's medical material, Erasmus's intention being to write a medical text-book to 'unravel the theory of diseases' and thereby to help their treatment.

Erasmus propounded in *Zoonomia* a theory of evolution which

34   Two plates from Erasmus Darwin's poem *The Botanic Garden*.

FLORA at play with CUPID.

Carl von Linné, or Linnaeus, who reclassified the plant kingdom.

resembled closely that of the great Lamarck who published fifteen years later, in 1809, his *Philosophie Zoologique*, in which he enunciated two laws. These were, in 1816, enlarged to a theory of four laws, which became in due course the great rival doctrine to that of Charles Darwin.

The essentials of Erasmus's doctrine of evolution are set forth in *Zoonomia* in the following words:

36

When we revolve in our minds, first, the great changes, which we see naturally produced in animals after their nativity, as in the production of the butterfly with painted wings from the crawling caterpillar; or of the respiring frog from the subnatant tadpole; from the feminine boy to the bearded man. ...

Secondly, when we think over the great changes introduced into various animals by artificial or accidental cultivation, as in horses, which we have exercised for the different purposes of strength or swiftness, in

The title page of Linnaeus's *Flora Lapponica (Flora of Lapland)*.

37

J. B. de Lamarck, who formulated one of the earliest theories of evolution, known to the French as the *Fondateur de l'Evolution*.

carrying burthens or in running races; or in dogs, which have been cultivated for strength and courage, as the bull-dog; or for acuteness of his sense of smell, as the hound and spaniel; or for the swiftness of his foot as the greyhound; or for his swimming in the water, or for drawing snow-sledges, and rough-haired dogs of the north ... and add to these the great change of shape and colour, which we daily see produced in smaller animals from our domestication of them, as rabbits, or pigeons; or from the difference of climates and even of seasons; thus the sheep of warm climates are covered with hair instead of wool; and the hares and partridges of the latitudes, which are long buried in snow, become white during the winter months. ...

Thirdly, when we enumerate the great changes produced in the species of animals before their nativity; these are such as resembles the form or colour of their parents, which have been altered by the cultivation or accidents above related, and are thus continued to their posterity. ...

Fourthly, when we revolve in our minds the great similarity of struc-

38

ture, which obtains in all the warm-blooded animals, as well as quadrupeds, birds and amphibious animals, as in mankind; from the mouse and bat to the elephant and whale; one is led to conclude that they have alike been produced from a similar living filament. ...

Fifthly, from their first rudiment, or primordium, to the termination of their lives, all animals undergo perpetual transformations which are in part produced by their own exertion in consequence of their desires and aversions, of their pleasures and their pains, or of imitations, or of associations; and many of these acquired forms or propensities are transmitted to their posterity.

When Erasmus speaks of perpetual transformation, he is anticipating Lamarck who insisted that the mechanism of evolution depended on the wishes and needs of the animals.

We approach the year 1809, when Charles Darwin was born and Lamarck's *Philosophie Zoologique* was published. The Jardin des Plantes in Paris has a large statue of Lamarck bearing the inscription, *'Fondateur de l'Evolution'*. This suggests, perhaps, that the English and French differ as to what is meant by evolution or as to whom to ascribe the credit for propounding the evolutionary doctrines which are accepted today.

The essence of Lamarck's theory was that changes in the condition of life produced changes in the needs of the animals affected. The new needs produced new habits and the new habits themselves change old structures or develop new ones. New organs may arise by the animal's own desires (*'sentiment intérieur'*) to meet the new circumstances. These changes in bodily form are then transmitted from parents to offspring and the species evolves. A simple example of this theory is that of the giraffe whose *'sentiment intérieur'* leads to the lengthening of its neck in order to get at higher leaves and whose lengthened neck is then inherited by its descendants.

For Lamarck, who incidentally invented the word 'biology', the real cause of evolutionary changes springs from an animal's behaviour – from its changing habits rather than from changes in the environment. Lamarck's ideas were suppressed by Cuvier, the greatest of comparative anatomists, who dominated European zoology for many years. In the evolutionary context, Cuvier appears today as the arch-reactionary. He insisted on the fixity of both species and varieties, that no living beings had changed since the creation.

At the end of the eighteenth century, therefore, in spite of the brilliant and suggestive ideas on the subject of the evolutionary

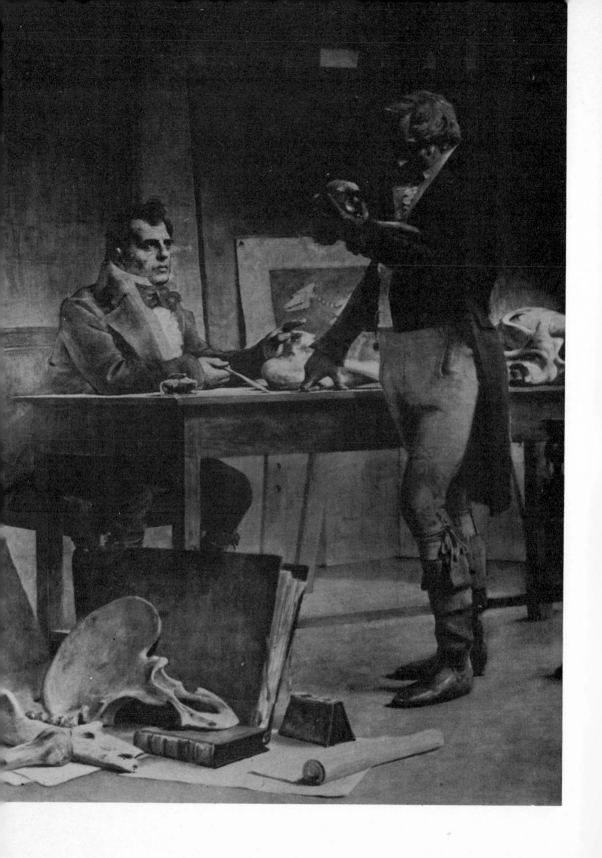

process of living things by Erasmus and Lamarck, discussions about evolution came to a halt. The opponents were too powerful; Coleridge and his friends had managed to attach the expression 'Darwinizing' to wild and eccentric fancies; Cuvier, the 'dictator of biology' had silenced Lamarck, and the Church, in England and abroad, was waiting to prosecute for blasphemy anyone who might, in his writings, treat man as an animal.

Although Erasmus and Lamarck may be called Darwinians of the old school, it is interesting that Charles Darwin did not take their ideas as the starting point for his evolutionary theories. Quite the contrary! He went out of his way to belittle their influence upon him and he began, as we shall see, quite afresh.

Let us bid farewell to the irrepressible Erasmus with his own magnificent vision of evolution taken from *Zoonomia*:

Would it be too bold to imagine, that in the great length of time, since the earth began to exist, perhaps million of ages before the commencement of the history of mankind, would it be too bold to imagine, that all warm-blooded animals have arisen from one living filament, which the *great first cause* endowed with animality, with the power of acquiring new parts, attended with new propensities, directed by imitations, sensations, volitions, and associations; and thus possessing this faculty of continuing to improve by its own inherent activity, and of delivering down those improvements by generation to its posterity, world without end!

OPPOSITE Baron Cuvier, the 'dictator' of biology, who suppressed the evolutionary views of Lamarck.

2
Father
and Son

THE STORY UNFOLDS in the west Midlands. Robert, Erasmus's son, married Susannah, Josiah Wedgwood's eldest daughter, in 1796. He had already been practising as a doctor at Shrewsbury for ten years and he had built up a successful practice.

But for this marriage, the Darwins and Wedgwoods might well have drifted apart. After Josiah's death in 1795, the family disbanded; Etruria Hall was put up for sale and his son and heir, Josiah, bought an estate in Dorset, where he did his best to set himself up as a rich country gentleman. His father had left over half a million pounds, as well as his large and flourishing business. Most of this fortune went to his son Josiah, his daughters each getting as a dowry £25,000. Circumstances, however, forced Josiah to return to Staffordshire and the pottery; the Napoleonic wars, and the Continental blockade in particular, were having a deleterious effect on his business; he had been living above his considerable means; moreover, try as he might – he travelled in a carriage-and-four attended by postillions in scarlet liveries and he became Sheriff of Dorset – he never made much social headway in Dorset society, which regarded him as a tradesman. Today, in our corrupt society, such vulgarity and *arrivisme* would excite admiration tinged with envy.

Josiah, then, returned to Staffordshire. Borrowing money from his new brother-in-law, Robert Darwin, he bought Maer Hall, seven miles from the Etruria Works. As another of his brothers-in-law, Sir James Mackintosh, said, 'A Wedgwood living out of Staffordshire must lose something of his proper importance.'

Despite the veneration in which he was held by his son Charles, Robert Darwin does not appear, from what one reads, to have been a very attractive character. The pictures of him in middle age show a gross, surly, pudding-faced creature; he became, indeed, an enormous man – the largest, said his son Charles, that he had ever seen. Out of this vast frame came a small, squeaky, rapid voice. He was dominating and unlovable. His bulk alone had an inhibiting effect on his family; when he came into a room, conversation stopped. Despite Robert Darwin's kindness and good-nature, no one ever felt at ease in his presence. He had to hear what everyone was saying – his daughter-in-law Emma, who later married Charles, described how he would say, 'Hm, hm, what is Emma saying?' Having effectively stopped any conversation, he would then impose his own vehement views on the company. Life in his household was highly disciplined; everything had to be correct and orderly and everyone had to conform to the Doctor's ideas.

PREVIOUS PAGES Charles Darwin, aged seven, with his sister Catherine, from a contemporary chalk drawing.

44

Dr Robert Waring Darwin,
the stern father of Charles.
The engraving by Thomas
Lupton is after a portrait by
James Pardon.

Although Charles always spoke of his father in terms of almost
oriental ancestor worship – his vast bulk the repository of omnis-
cience and God-like wisdom – he liked nothing more than to
escape, with his brother and sisters, to the carefree atmosphere of
of the Wedgwoods' home at Maer.

A year or two after his marriage, Robert built a house, The
Mount, just outside Shrewsbury on the Welsh side of the river. It
is a solid, red-brick house of Georgian design, the main feature
being the splendid view over the River Severn. Robert planted the

45

garden with fruit trees and ornamental shrubs and this was as near as he ever got to taking an interest in natural history.

It was in this house that Charles Darwin was born on 12 February 1809. His parents had six children, two boys and four girls, and Charles was the youngest but one. His elder brother, Erasmus, born five years earlier, died a bachelor at the age of seventy-seven. Always solitary and unwell, his gentle and refined personality drew people to him. Charles often spoke of him later as 'Poor old

The Mount, the house built by Robert Darwin just outside Shrewsbury shortly after his marriage, where Charles was born.

46

Ras' or 'Poor dear old Philos' – a reminder of the days when they worked at chemistry together in the tool shed at The Mount. Charles's daughter once described the warmth of his welcome to his nephews and nieces at his home in Queen Anne Street: 'We came into that simply furnished, somewhat ascetic London drawing-room, looking out on the bare street, knowing that he was weary and ill, and had been alone, and would be alone again, and yet went away with a glow reflected from his atmosphere – a sense that the world was better for his presence.'

Charles's mother, Susannah, the eldest of the great Josiah Wedgwood's children, was possessed of many virtues and accomplishments. She was her father's favourite child and she gave music lessons to her future father-in-law Erasmus Darwin, who admitted that his learning and talents did not extend to this particular art. She made, however, very little impression upon her son Charles, who is brutally frank about the indistinctness of his memories of her. He was eight when she died in 1817 at the rather uninteresting age of fifty-two. 'It is odd', said Charles, 'that I can hardly remember anything about her except her deathbed, her black velvet gown, and her curiously constructed work-table.'

Charles made good, it seems, this want of affection for his mother and her memory by an inordinate attachment to his monolithic father. Whenever, in later life, he spoke about him, he generally prefaced his remarks with, 'My father, who was the wisest man I knew'.

More clearly than his mother's death, Charles remembered the illuminations after the Battle of Waterloo and the militia exercising outside his father's house. He claimed that his very first memory was when, at the age of four, he was sitting in the drawing-room on his sister Caroline's knee; she was cutting an orange for him and, as she did so, a cow ran by the window making him jump and thereby receive a bad cut, the scar from which he bore for the rest of his life.

In 1817, when he was eight-and-a-half years old, Charles went to a day-school at Shrewsbury kept by the Reverend G. Case, Minister of the Unitarian Chapel. His mother was a Unitarian and worshipped in this Chapel, occasionally taking Charles and his elder sisters with her.

Already by this time, Charles's taste for natural history and, even more, for collecting was well developed. He fished for newts in the quarry pool and collected such things as seals, franks, coins and minerals. He was fond of gardening and botanizing and he

48   A view of Shrewsbury and the countryside where Darwin spent his childhood.

invented a story, to impress some other small boys, that he was able to produce differently coloured crocuses and polyanthuses by watering them with coloured fluids. In some recollections, written towards the end of his life, he mentioned this episode as testifying to his early interest in the variability of plants. Apart from this and one or two other tall stories, his main memories during his year with Dr Case were of gardening, collecting things, travelling with his father in his carriage and admiring game and other wild birds. 'I was', he said, 'a born naturalist.' One other episode impressed itself on his mind – the burial of a dragoon soldier: 'It is surprising how clearly I can still see the horse with the man's empty boots and carbine suspended to the saddle, and the firing over the grave. This scene deeply stirred whatever poetic fancy there was in me.'

In 1818, Charles went to the Shrewsbury Grammar School. He stayed there seven years, until 1825, and summed up the usefulness of the education which he received there as follows: 'Nothing could have been worse for the development of my mind than Dr Butler's school, as it was strictly classical, nothing else being taught, except a little ancient geography and history. The school as a means of education to me was a complete blank.' The Reverend Samuel Butler had been appointed headmaster of Shrewsbury School in 1798. It had, in the sixteenth century, been one of the leading schools in the country, but had declined under a series of mediocre headmasters. By the end of the eighteenth century, the school had reached the nadir of its reputation and few Shrewsbury parents thought any longer of sending their sons there as boarders. There was talk about the school folding up until, at the last minute, St John's College, Cambridge, who held the gift of appointing the headmaster, nominated Samuel Butler. He was only twenty-four and a Fellow of St John's, where he had had a singularly brilliant career in classics and mathematics. He remained headmaster of Shrewsbury for thirty-eight years and the school acquired during those years a very high reputation. His life was later written by his grandson, Samuel Butler, author of *The Way of all Flesh*.

Dr Butler's methods of restoring the school's reputation were competitive examination and discipline, which meant intensive instruction in Greek and Latin, and flogging. It is curious that Charles should have benefited so little from the education which he received at the hands of the distinguished Dr Butler. All he admitted to enjoying were the Odes of Horace and Shakespeare's

Shrewsbury Grammar School – a sketch by C. W. Radclyffe.

Dr Samuel Butler, whose tuition made little impact on Darwin and who failed to see any evidence of genius in him.

history plays, which he read for hours on end in an old window in the thick walls of the school. He hated verse-making and just got by with the help of other boys. He learned the necessary number of lines from Homer and Virgil in morning chapel and forgot them forty-eight hours later. Apart from a little geography and ancient history, nothing else was taught. It is not surprising, then, that Dr Butler had a low opinion of Charles's abilities. This was not modified when he learned that Charles and his elder brother Erasmus conducted chemical experiments in their toolshed. He rebuked him in public for wasting his time in this way and the other boys nicknamed him 'Gas'.

52

Although The Mount was only a mile away from the school, Robert Darwin sent both his sons there as boarders. Charles later said that he thereby 'had the great advantage of leading the life of a true schoolboy'. The boys slept two in a bed; for an extra fee, a boy could have a bed to himself.

Charles remembered himself as being in those days passionate and quarrelsome: 'I swore like a trooper.' Outside the classroom, he continued his natural history pursuits, collecting pebbles and beetles. After reading Gilbert White's *The Natural History of Selborne,* he studied the habits of birds and wondered why every gentleman did not become an ornithologist.

Robert shared Dr Butler's low view of Charles's attainments and removed him from school prematurely at the age of sixteen, telling him, 'You care for nothing but shooting, dogs and rat-catching, and you will be a disgrace to yourself and all your family.' Charles called this decision 'wise' and explained away these unpleasant remarks with: 'My father, who was the kindest man I ever knew and whose memory I love with all my heart, must have been angry and somewhat unjust when he used such words.' Robert decided to send Charles to Edinburgh University to study medicine. He wanted him to become a doctor. In fact, he wanted both his sons to become doctors. Erasmus had earlier gone to Cambridge and was now going to Edinburgh, the plan being that Charles should accompany him.

Our picture of Charles Darwin at the age of sixteen is one of a cheerful, happy, sweet-tempered, unambitious boy, not unduly perturbed by his indifferent achievements at school or by his father's disapproval. His love of observation and experiment, whether in the tool-shed or in the open air; his fondness for the outdoor life, whether riding in the Welsh countryside or shooting with his cousins in Staffordshire, may have compensated for the bleaker aspects of his life at home and at school.

Why did Robert fail so completely to recognize any lurking elements of genius in his son? Why did he wish to thrust upon him the distasteful practice of medicine? He himself admitted that he had at first hated the profession and would have left it if his father had given him any other choice; he could never endure the sight of blood. His early memories of the medical profession could not have been all that happy, since his elder brother Charles had died of a wound which occurred when he was dissecting the brain of a child. And yet, this crassly unimaginative colossus, who never attempted to understand his son's gifts, and whose life, as

ABOVE Edinburgh University, where Darwin studied medicine, but became more interested in zoology.

OPPOSITE The College Hall at Edinburgh.

we shall see later, he very nearly ruined by refusing to let him go on his historic journey round the world, must have had something nice about him to be able to arouse in his son such sustained and unqualified love and admiration.

Writers about Darwin will no doubt say, or have already said, that his life can be described as one long struggle with his father; he wished both to please him and to defer to his judgment, and yet disliked the two alternative careers his father had chosen for him — medicine or the Church. He wanted, for some reason or other, his father's approval, but did not know how to secure it. It would be possible to explain other phenomena in his life by reference to the father-son relationship; for example, that he put off for twenty years or more the publication of his findings about evolution for fear that he might offend his formidable father, giving his real or supposed ill-health as one of the reasons. All this is conjectural and

54

does not get us very far. Despite Charles's unbounded admiration for his father's wisdom and his intuitive judgment of men and women, he was objective about his abilities:

My father's mind was not scientific, and he did not try to generalise his knowledge under general laws; yet he formed a theory for almost everything which occurred. I do not think I gained much from him intellectually; but his example ought to have been of much moral service to all his children. One of his golden rules (a hard one to follow) was, 'Never become the friend of any one whom you cannot respect.'

Why Charles should have found such a rule hard to follow is curious.

So Charles went to Edinburgh in 1825 to train to be a doctor, as his grandfather Erasmus had done seventy years earlier. His own brother Erasmus was on the point of finishing his medical studies, which he had been half-heartedly pursuing. Charles later disarmingly admitted that he had made no strenuous effort to learn medicine at Edinburgh because 'I became convinced that my father would leave me property enough to subsist on with some comfort. ...'

Once again, Charles took little interest in his set studies. He decided that lectures were a waste of time. 'To my mind there are no advantages and many disadvantages in lectures compared with reading.' Nevertheless, lectures in Edinburgh were compulsory; he described Dr Andrew Duncan's lectures on *Materia Medica* at eight o'clock on winter mornings as 'something fearful to remember.' As for Dr Alexander Munro, 'he made his lectures on human

anatomy as dull as he was himself and the subject disgusted me'. Charles found that he was squeamish in the operating theatre; he attended two operations, one on a child, and ran away in the middle. The memory of them haunted him for many years. He resolved never again to be present at an operation, this being long before 'the blessed days of chloroform'. He later bitterly regretted that he was not urged at this time to practise dissection, which would have been so useful to him later as a naturalist. This and his inability to draw were, in his view, two irremediable evils. Charles quite enjoyed, although not as much as he thought he would, the clinical lectures in the hospitals, taking the patients as the subjects. It reminded him how he had, the summer before, picked up a few patients among the poor at Shrewsbury. He had written down their symptoms and then read them aloud to his father, who advised what medicines to give.

The lectures apart, Charles was reasonably happy in Edinburgh. Like all visitors, he admired the beauty of the town and the friendliness of its inhabitants. He and his brother found two bedrooms and a sitting-room in Lothian Street.

Edinburgh turned out not to be a complete waste of time. Erasmus left after a year and Charles then made some friends who were interested in natural science. Of these new friends, two, John Coldstream and Robert Grant, introduced him to the practical study of marine zoology. Coldstream was a straight-laced, religious young man who later published zoological articles. Grant was older and already of a certain zoological eminence; he later became the first professor of zoology in University College, London. Charles thought him dry and formal, 'with much enthusiasm beneath the outer crust'. It was their habit to go off on zoological walks together, collecting, and later dissecting, animals from tidal pools. One day, on one of these walks, Grant 'burst forth in high admiration of Lamarck and his views on evolution'. Charles listened with surprise and recognised the similarity of these views to those of his grandfather in *Zoonomia*, which had not made any impression upon him. He was impressed by the fact that Grant should take seriously the evolutionary theories of Lamarck and his grandfather. This may well have been the moment, as he later suggested, when evolution started to grip his scientific imagination.

Charles went out trawling for oysters with Newhaven fishermen and thus got a good many specimens. In spite of his lack of dissecting skill and having only an inadequate microscope, he made a

56

modest discovery and read a paper on it before the Plinian Society of Edinburgh. 'This was that the so-called ova of Flustra (sea-mat) had the power of independent movement by means of cilia, and were in fact larvae.'

The happiest moments of Charles's student days were those spent at Maer with the Wedgwoods, where the atmosphere was more carefree than at The Mount. There he indulged his obsessive enjoyment of shooting: 'My zeal was so great that I used to place my shooting-boots open by my bedside when I went to bed, so as not to lose half a minute in putting them on in the morning.' He thought nothing of reaching a remote part of The Maer estate when it was still dark and toiling all day with the gamekeeper through thick heath and young Scotch firs. He kept an exact record of every bird he shot throughout the season. For each bird he made a knot in a piece of string tied to his button-hole.

Apart from the shooting, there were many other things about Maer to delight the mind and the senses. The spacious Elizabethan house was set in pleasing countryside which contained a good deal of heath and woods enclosing a garden 'landscaped' by Capability Brown. The house took its name from a small lake, or mere, which Capability Brown had made the main feature of the garden. The Wedgwood children boated and skated on it, according to the season. They all retained a kind of sacred feeling about Maer – and none more so than Emma, the ninth and young-est child of Josiah and Elizabeth Wedgwood. Charles, who was later to marry her, spoke idyllically about Maer:

Life there was perfectly free; the country was very pleasant for walk-ing or riding; and in the evening there was much very agreeable conver-sation, not so personal as it generally is in larger family parties, together with music. In the summer, the whole family used often to sit on the steps of the old portico, with the flower-garden in front, and with the steep wooded bank opposite the house reflected in the lake, with here and there a fish rising or a water-bird paddling about. Nothing has left a more vivid picture on my mind than these evenings at Maer.

During his second year at Edinburgh, Charles decided that he definitely did not want to be a doctor, but nor did he know what he wanted to do. The only alternative his father could think of was the Church, which might, at any rate, prevent him from degenerat-ing into an idle sportsman. Charles compliantly agreed. He proceeded to read one or two divinity books and was quite satis-fied about 'the strict and literal truth of every word in the Bible'. He probably pictured himself in some quiet country parish with

OVERLEAF Christ's College, Cambridge. Darwin con-sidered his time there 'sadly wasted' though he admitted that he had enjoyed it.

plenty of time for studying local natural history. Gilbert White's *Selborne* had been, after all, one of his favourite books as a child.

To be a clergyman it was necessary to have a university degree and to know the Classics. Charles discovered that, in the two years since he had left school, he had forgotten almost all his Latin and Greek, even the Greek alphabet. Instead of going up to Cambridge in October 1827, he crammed at The Mount with a tutor and found that he was able by the end of the year to translate Homer and the Greek New Testament reasonably easily.

Charles went up to Christ's College, Cambridge, at the beginning of 1828:

My time was sadly wasted there, and worse than wasted. From my passion for shooting and for hunting, and, when this failed, for riding across country, I got into a sporting set, including some dissipated low-minded young men. We used often to dine together in the evening, though these dinners often included men of a higher stamp, and we sometimes drank too much, with jolly singing and playing at cards afterwards. I know that I ought to feel ashamed of days and evenings thus spent, but as some of my friends were very pleasant, and we were all in the highest spirits, I cannot help looking back to these times with much pleasure.

These were Charles's comments on his three years at Cambridge. As far as the academic studies were concerned, his performance was as indifferent as it had been at Edinburgh and at school.

Although it is possible that Charles, as his son Francis Darwin later suggested, liked to exaggerate the dissipated quality of his life at Cambridge, it is clear that he took things very easily. Christ's was a sporting college suited to well-off sons of country gentlemen and Charles fitted naturally into this setting. At the age of nineteen, when he went up to Cambridge, he was a tall, slender young man, with pale blue eyes, a broad flattish nose, a heavy brow and a captivatingly serene and gentle expression. He was immensely popular with his friends and he called the three years which he spent at Cambridge 'the most joyful in my happy life; for I was then in excellent health and almost always in high spirits'.

Charles's life at Cambridge was not given over entirely to activities associated with the sporting set. It is true that he spent a good deal of his time lounging about in the Gourmet Club – drinking and card-playing – and indulging out of doors in more virile 'horsey' activities, such as riding. But his artistic sensibilities, which were then, as throughout his life, limited, began to show slight signs of developing. One of his friends 'inoculated'

OPPOSITE Darwin; at this period of his life he was an active sportsman.

61

him with a taste for pictures and engravings and he bought a few to decorate his rooms in Christ's. He often visited the Fitzwilliam Museum and he claimed that his taste must have been good, as he unfailingly admired the best pictures. Charles also found himself, to his surprise, in a musical set: 'I am so utterly destitute of an ear, that I cannot perceive a discord, or keep time and hum a tune correctly; and it is a mystery how I could possibly have derived pleasure from music.' Nevertheless, he used to go to King's College Chapel to hear the anthems; these gave him such intense pleasure as to cause his backbone to shiver. He also hired the choir boys to sing in his rooms.

There are no other signs of the emergence of new intellectual or artistic interests. Charles did the bare minimum of work on classics and mathematics needed for the ordinary degree, in which he came tenth in the 'poll' of January 1831. The only parts of the course, the study of which had any effect on his mind, were, so he believed, Euclid and Paley's *Evidences*. William Paley's *Evidences of Christianity*, published in 1794, is an admirably clear text-book of Anglican orthodoxy. Charles was delighted with its logic, which he found as convincing as Euclid.

From all accounts, Charles was, at this period of his life, a most invigorating and attractive person. His contemporaries speak of his pleasant looks, his energy and geniality, his humour and simplicity, his generous sympathy 'with all that was good and true' and his hatred of anything mean or cruel. It is difficult to associate this full-blooded young man – his gallops across country, *vingt-et-un* suppers, shooting in the fens – with the melancholy, shawl-covered old hypochondriac of later years.

Although he was academically indolent, Charles's love for natural history was steadily increasing: 'No pursuit at Cambridge was followed with nearly so much eagerness or gave me so much pleasure as collecting beetles.' Charles became an indefatigable collector of beetles and amassed a large and valuable collection. He paid a man to scrape moss off old trees in winter and to collect rubbish from the barges which brought the reeds from the fens; he thereby got some rare species. One of his proudest moments was when he saw the words 'captured by C. Darwin' in L. Stephens's *Illustrations of British Entomology*.

The most important feature of Charles's life at Cambridge was his friendship with J.S. Henslow, the young professor of botany. His enthusiasm for botany infected many of the undergraduates. Charles became his constant companion and was known to the

H. W. Pickering's drawing of
Sir John Herschel. His
*Introduction to the Study of
Natural Philosophy* was
another book which
influenced Darwin.

dons as 'the man who walks with Henslow'. Henslow advised
Charles to read Alexander von Humboldt's *Personal Narrative of
Travels to the Equinoctial Regions of America* and Sir John Herschel's
Introduction to the Study of Natural Philosophy. These two books
had an electric effect on Charles. Humboldt made him want to go
then and there to see for himself the glories of Teneriffe, and
Herschel's book 'stirred up in me a burning zeal to add even the
most humble contribution to the noble structure of natural
science'.

Another of Henslow's achievements was to persuade Charles to
overcome his aversion to geology. He introduced him to Adam
Sedgwick, professor of geology at Cambridge, with whom he
shortly afterwards went on a geological tour of North Wales. He
had earlier, towards the end of his Cambridge career, with Henslow's encouragement, started a systematic investigation of local
rocks, making maps and analysing sections. This had given him a
rudimentary preparation for his outing with Sedgwick. The latter
was one of the great leaders in the heroic age of geology. He had an
extraordinary power of unravelling the stratigraphy of a complicated district and of recognizing which were the important facts to
support a theory. Charles noticed, however, that he was disconcerted when some unexpected fact threatened to disturb a care-

fully formulated theory. When they were staying at The Mount during their tour, a local workman produced a tropical shell which he had found in a gravel pit. Charles was excited by this unusual find; Sedgwick, on the other hand, was irritated and put out, saying that it would be a great misfortune to geology if it turned out that the shell really *had* been embedded in the pit, 'as it would overthrow all that we know about the superficial deposits of the Midland Counties'. Sedgwick was later strongly opposed to Charles's hypothesis about the origin of species. This episode brought home to Charles for the first time that science consisted of grouping together certain facts so that general laws or conclusions could be drawn from them.

Charles left Sedgwick near Bangor in order to join some Cambridge friends at Barmouth for a reading party. He then went on to Maer for the shooting. The partridge season was about to start and 'at that time I should have thought myself mad to give up the first days of partridge shooting for geology or any other science'.

BELOW Adam Sedgwick, the professor of geology whom Darwin met at Cambridge.

OVERLEAF Etruria Hall, 1780: Sarah and Josiah Wedgwood (seated together on the right) with their family. Susannah, later Darwin's mother, is on horseback (centre).

3 The Beagle

O N MONDAY 29 AUGUST 1831, Charles dropped in at The Mount on his way to Maer for the partridge shooting. He found awaiting him a letter in an unfamiliar hand; it was from George Peacock, professor of anatomy at Cambridge, and it enclosed another letter to Charles from his friend Henslow. In it, Peacock offered him the post of unpaid naturalist on board HMS *Beagle* and companion to the Captain, Robert FitzRoy. Peacock possessed the authority of nominating naturalists to ships making surveys and, on this occasion, had asked Henslow to recommend someone. The British Government had decided to complete the survey of the South American coast, which had been begun several years before. The *Beagle*, a six-gun brig, was chosen for the purpose and Captain FitzRoy was given the command.

Henslow told Charles that he considered him the best qualified person for such a post:

I state this not in the supposition of your being a *finished* naturalist, but as amply qualified for collecting, observing and noting, anything worthy to be noted in natural history ... don't put on any modest doubts or fears about your qualifications, for I assure you I think you are the very man they are in search of; so conceive yourself to be tapped on the shoulder by your bum-bailiff and affectionate friend. ...

Peacock also pressed Charles to accept the offer. The plan was, he said, for the ship to survey first the south coast of Tierra del Fuego, then the South Sea islands, and to return by the Indian Archipelago to England. The ship would sail at the end of September – in exactly a month. He described Captain FitzRoy as a nephew of the Duke of Grafton and 'a public-spirited and zealous officer, of delightful manners, and greatly beloved by all his brother officers'.

Charles's first thought was to leap at the offer. But he knew that he would be able to accept only if his father gave his approval. Robert Darwin came out strongly against the whole scheme. He saw Charles, once again, shifting his sights – this time away from the Church – and drifting irretrievably into a life of sport and idleness. Robert qualified his refusal with the words, 'If you can find any man of common sense who advises you to go I will give my consent.' It was enough for Charles to know that his father disapproved of his going on the expedition for him to write, on 30 August, to Henslow declining: 'My father, although he does not decidedly refuse me, gives such strong advice against going, that I should not be comfortable if I did not follow it.'

Nothing can illustrate better Charles's equable, easy-going

PREVIOUS PAGES HMS *Beagle* on the shores of the Santa Cruz River as members of the crew careen her.

OPPOSITE Robert FitzRoy, the *Beagle*'s temperamental captain, for whom Darwin retained a lasting affection.

71

nature than this docile act of submission to his father's wishes. It was the Wedgwoods who, when he arrived at Maer next day for the partridge shooting, were shocked that he should have rejected so magnificent an opportunity. Josiah Wedgwood offered himself as the 'man of common sense' who might persuade Robert Darwin to change his mind. The Wedgwood indignation emboldened Charles to write to Robert from Maer, attaching a letter from Josiah Wedgwood which answered effectively each of his father's objections to the proposed voyage. Robert's objections were, in Charles's words, as follows:

1. Disreputable to my character as a clergyman hereafter.
2. A wild scheme.
3. That they must have offered to many others before me the place of Naturalist.
4. And from its not being accepted there must be some serious objection to the vessel or expedition.
5. That I should never settle down to a steady life hereafter.
6. That my accommodation would be most uncomfortable.
7. That you, that is, Dr Darwin, should consider it as again changing my profession.
8. That it would be a useless undertaking.

Josiah's answers to the doctor's objections were sensible and convincing. 'Is is not the case that sailors are prone to settle in domestic and quiet habits?' (objection 5). He pointed out (objection 1) that the study of natural history was a very suitable activity for a clergyman. This was the prevailing view. Anglican clergymen tended to think of dogmatic Christianity as being improbable or silly; it was more rational and natural to look for God in the meadows and hedgerows, to admire the divine purposes in the growth of plants and the habits of insects. Gilbert White, author of the *Natural History of Selborne*, was for Englishmen the model of a country clergyman.

Robert was persuaded by Josiah's arguments and withdrew his opposition. Charles went hurriedly to Cambridge to see Henslow and to make certain that the post had not been given away. After spending a couple of days at Cambridge with Henslow, he went to London to meet FitzRoy. Charles was delighted with the meeting; he could not praise FitzRoy too highly. He wrote to Henslow, saying, 'Captain FitzRoy is everything that is delightful. If I were to praise him half as much as I fell inclined, you would say it was absurd, only once seeing him.' FitzRoy warned Charles of the cramped conditions on board the *Beagle*, of the dangers of being

72

thrown too closely together for a three-year voyage. However, he offered to share his cabin with him and to make him as comfortable as possible.

Charles was later to learn that there were many oddities about FitzRoy's character. He studied physiognomy and very nearly turned Charles down because of the shape of his nose. The Darwins had broad, squat noses and FitzRoy doubted whether anyone with such a nose could have the character and determination to survive an arduous sea voyage. The enforced intimacy of these two young men – Charles was twenty-two and FitzRoy twenty-three when

Conrad Martens, who replaced Augustus Earle as artist aboard the *Beagle*. He was, according to Darwin, 'a pleasant person, and like all birds of that class, full up to the mouth with enthusiasm'. He joined the ship at Montevideo.

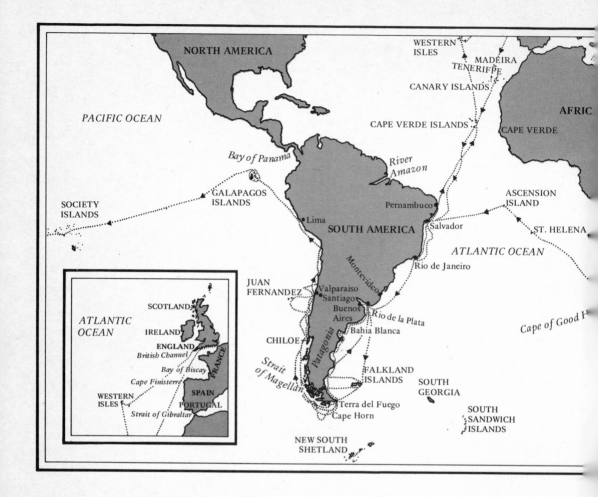

the *Beagle* set sail on 27 December 1821 – during what turned out to be a five-year journey round the world must have left certain marks upon Charles. It was not long before he qualified his starry-eyed description of FitzRoy's virtues.

FitzRoy was handsome, courteous and aristocratic in his bearing. He had the saturnine good looks of Charles II, from whom he was descended through the King's liaison with Barbara Villiers, and the brooding, depressive temperament of his uncle, Lord Castlereagh, whose example he later followed by committing suicide. FitzRoy's views on life were authoritarian, conservative and cranky. He was a magnificent seaman and a stern disciplinarian. Charles was rather upset when, at the end of two miserable months of waiting at Plymouth for the ship to sail, FitzRoy had most of the crew flogged and put in heavy chains for drunkenness.

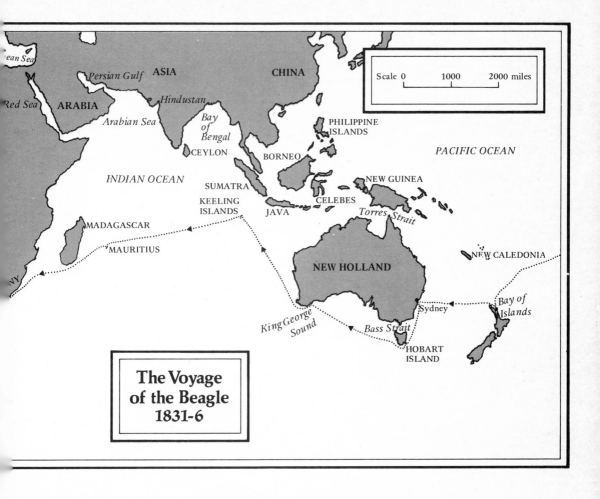

Scale 0   1000   2000 miles

PACIFIC OCEAN

PHILIPPINE
ISLANDS

ASIA   CHINA

Persian Gulf

Red Sea   ARABIA   Hindustan

Arabian Sea   Bay
of
Bengal

CEYLON   BORNEO

INDIAN OCEAN   SUMATRA

KEELING
ISLANDS   CELEBES

JAVA

NEW GUINEA

Torres Strait

MADAGASCAR

MAURITIUS   NEW CALEDONIA

NEW HOLLAND

Sydney   Bay of
Islands

King George
Sound   Bass Strait

HOBART
ISLAND

**The Voyage
of the Beagle
1831-6**

He disliked the callous side of FitzRoy's nature, which showed itself on various occasions. For instance, FitzRoy approved of slavery, which Charles, like his grandfather Erasmus before him, abominated. On one occasion during their journey, at Bahia in Brazil, FitzRoy said that he had just visited a great slave owner who had called up his slaves, one after the other, and asked them whether they were happy and if they wanted to be set free. They replied, in one voice, no. This, for FitzRoy, was an ample vindication of slavery. When Charles expressed his doubts as to the value of the slaves' testimony in the presence of their master, FitzRoy flew into a rage and said that they could no longer live together. Such was FitzRoy's excitable temperament.

Charles had a deep affection for this unbalanced man. He did not see much of him after their return home, largely because of the

The *Beagle* in South America

The *Beagle*'s first port of call was the Brazilian town of Bahia. Darwin was overwhelmed by the beauty of the tropical forests and vegetation of Brazil. These pictures show how natives, settlers and visitors lived there.

The Beagle *at Sydney Harbour* by Owen Stanley. A small ten-ton brig, she nevertheless had to accommodate seventy-four people and was fitted out at great expense with mahogany furnishings.

Owen Stanley

unpredictability of his temper. Furthermore, Charles's scientific reflections were leading him steadily further away from religious orthodoxy, whereas FitzRoy became more fixed in his fundamentalist views: 'He was afterwards very indignant with me for having published so unorthodox a book (for he became very religious) as *The Origin of Species*.' However, when FitzRoy left England to become Governor of New Zealand, Charles wrote to him, 'I cannot bear the thought of your leaving the country without seeing you once again; the past is often in my memory, and I feel that I owe to you much bygone enjoyment and the whole destiny of my life.'

HMS *Beagle* 'sailed from England on our circumnavigation' on 27 December 1831, and anchored at Falmouth five years later on 2 October 1836.

The voyage of the *Beagle* has been by far the most important event in my life, and has determined my whole career. ... Everything about which I thought or read was made to bear directly on what I had seen or was likely to see; and this habit of mind was continued during the five years of the voyage. I feel sure that this was a training which has enabled me to do whatever I have done in science.

This famous voyage has an inspiring and exhilarating quality which distinguishes it from other similar expeditions. In Charles's note-books, letters and journal, we witness the deepening and concentration of his processes of thought and the steady transformation of his personality. When he stepped onto the *Beagle*, he was a good-humoured, easy-going young man with little intellectual ambition, who dabbled in geology and collected beetles. He returned to England a formidable figure – according to his father, even the shape of his head had changed. He had found, once and for all, a channel for his energies, intellectual and emotional, the means of expressing his genius. The great design of his life began to take shape – the explanation of the origins of living creatures. His earlier pastimes, such as shooting and collecting, were now made to serve his new scientific purposes. In addition to his developing gifts of detailed investigation and theorizing from observed facts, Charles experienced during the journey a near religious fervour for all aspects of nature, whether the structure of a fragment of rock or the mystery of the tropical forest. He had greater opportunities for studying and admiring the variety and grandeur of God's works than had young men at home who were destined for the Church. He began to search for the underlying causes of all the strange and beautiful things he saw, whether animate or inanimate; this was a search which was to continue, with increasing ardour and concentration, for the rest of his life and to earn him the title of 'the Newton of biology'.

The object of the *Beagle* voyage was, as Charles briefly put it, 'to complete the survey of Patagonia and Tierra del Fuego, commenced under Captain King in 1826 to 1830; to survey the shores of Chile, Peru, and some islands in the Pacific; and to carry a chain of chronometrical measurements round the world'. She weighed 235 tons and belonged to the old class of ten-gun brigs, known as 'coffins' because they tended to sink in bad weather. Charles said that he learned his methodical working habits from the cramped space on board the *Beagle*: 'I have just room to turn round, and that is all.' He suffered acutely from sea-sickness: 'The real misery begins when you are so exhausted that a little exertion makes a feeling of faintness come on.' All he could eat were raisins, which his father had recommended. It has been suggested that his later ill-health was due to these sufferings, although Charles ascribed it either to a hereditary fault, which took the form of gout in earlier days, or to a severe illness which he contracted in South America, now thought to be Chagas's Disease.

Charles's first account of his journey round the world on the *Beagle* was published in 1839 with the title *Journal of researches into the geology and natural history of the various countries visited by H.M.S. Beagle* etc. This had been earlier published as the third volume of a set entitled *The narrative of the voyages of H.M. Ships Adventure and Beagle* edited by Captain FitzRoy. The publisher John Murray quickly saw that Charles's contribution to the official account of the voyage had the makings of a best-seller. This proved, indeed, to be the case; the *Journal of Researches* has taken its place as one of the most absorbing travel books in our literature and there have been almost a hundred reissues and new editions since it was first published.

It is interesting that the word 'geology' preceded 'natural history' in the title of the first edition of the *Journal of Researches*. This is no doubt because geology was uppermost in Charles's mind at the time. His interest in the subject had been, as we have seen, stimulated by Henslow and Sedgwick. It became a passion when he started to read Charles Lyell's great book *Principles of Geology* which had recently appeared. Henslow forwarded to Charles the volumes as they were published, advising him, however, 'to take no notice of his theories'. What Henslow objected to were Lyell's anti-cataclysmic arguments. It was Lyell's book

John Murray, Darwin's publisher, who realized the potential public interest in Darwin's account of his researches during the voyage.

which, more than anything else, released the creative springs of Charles's thought during the journey. The impact on his mind of Lyell's daring theories, vivified by his astonishing new daily experiences of mountain chains, tropical forests and volcanic reefs, caused Charles to feel within himself the stirrings of greatness. He was now fired with the new vision of Lyell and he would, in due course, direct this new-found vision towards other phenomena of nature and become the mighty intellectual force of the nineteenth century.

Lyell's *Principles* gave the death-blow to the catastrophic school of geologists. The Catastrophists, as they were called, had simple, clear-cut explanations for the changes which the earth and its inhabitants had undergone during the previous few thousand years. Their leader was the great Cuvier in France and their authority was the Bible. The Catastrophic Theory taught that there had been a series of floods in the past, when the earth was covered by sea and all living things drowned. The different layers of fossils represented the life destroyed by such cataclysms, of which Noah's flood was the most recent. Life consisted, therefore, of a series of repeated acts of creation and destruction. The Almighty destroyed in His wrath what He had in His mercy created. The new species which God made were in no way related to the victims of earlier floods. They were fixed, solid and immutable, like those species which Adam found in Paradise and which still exist today – apart, of course, from those which Man, and no longer God, is killing off.

Linnaeus, the Swedish professor at Uppsala, assumed the formidable task of classifying all those animals and plants which had been obediently multiplying themselves since the days of Adam. He gave to each a specific and generic name. His system did not allow for the inclusion of 'extinct' species. Since his death, several strange skeletons had been found, which did not resemble any living animals. There was the giant sloth, or Megatherium, in South America; a mammoth corpse was found in Siberia with curved tusks and a red woolly coat. Where did these extinct species come from? Was it possible that they had died out since the last flood? Cuvier and the Catastrophists explained that they belonged to an earlier creation, with which Adam had had nothing to do. There had been a long series of periods in the earth's history, each with its distinct set of plants and animals.

Lyell showed in his book that this account of alternating creation and destruction was rubbish. He was anticipated by the

OPPOSITE Charles Lyell, the distinguished Scottish geologist, was one of the first scientists to refute the earlier theories of creation, in his *Principles of Geology*.

The giant sloth (Mega-
therium): a skeleton had been
found in the Argentine and
sent to Madrid fifty years
previously. Darwin collected
as many fossilized skeletons
of extinct animals as possible
and shipped them home.

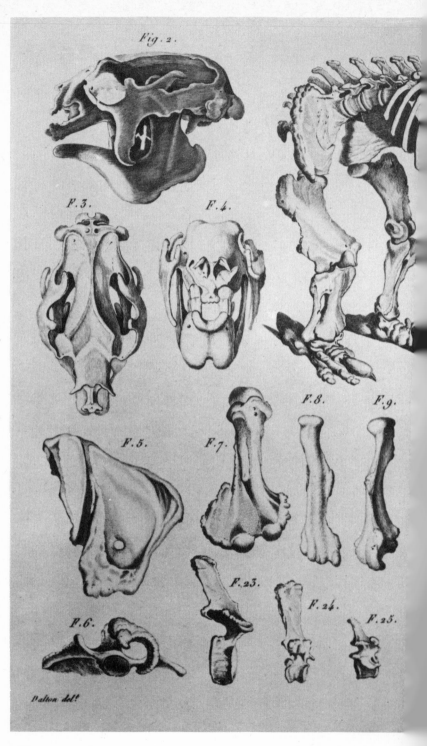

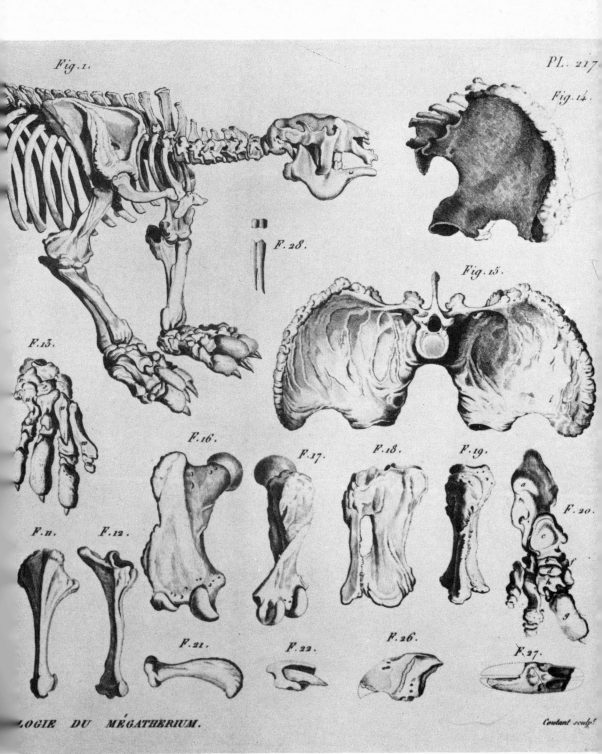

Fig. 1.

PL. 217.

Fig. 14.

F. 28.

Fig. 15.

F. 13.

F. 16.

F. 17.

F. 18.

F. 19.

F. 20.

F. 11.

F. 12.

F. 21.

F. 22.

F. 26.

F. 27.

...LOGIE DU MÉGATHERIUM.

Coutant sculp.

The ancient town of Bahia in San Salvador, set on a hill with waving palms: this was Darwin's first glimpse of Brazil, engraved here from an impression by Augustus Earle.

Edinburgh geologist James Hutton who published in 1785 *The Theory of the Earth*. He had pointed out both the volcanic origin of many rocks and the action of rivers in carving out valleys. He said that the earth, as we know it today, had been formed by causes working very gradually over an immense period of time. His followers were called the Uniformitarians and they joined battle with the Catastrophists. Lyell became converted to Uniformitarianism when he saw the effect of the sea's erosion of the Norfolk coast. It was his convincing exposition of the continuous

action of natural causes acting over vast periods of time which had so great an influence on Charles during the *Beagle* voyage. It was Lyell's book that led him to apply the principles of evolution in geology to animal life.

There was no need for God and His high-handed ways in Lyell's geology. The changes in the earth's surface were not brought about by catastrophes, but occurred in the course of millions of years. The catastrophe theory in geology had been discredited; it remained, nevertheless, true that species *had* been destroyed. If

87

they had died out slowly and naturally, new species might equally have arisen slowly and naturally. There might even have been a tenuous link between this natural extinction and this natural new-birth or origin. Some of the old species might have been transformed into new ones. Lyell had shown that terrestrial things are constantly changing, even without catastrophes – water, land, valleys and even the climate. Could living organisms be affected by these slow changes in their environment or habitats? Some species might be unable to adapt themselves and therefore die out; others might adjust themselves to new conditions by developing new forms – in fact, a transformation of species could occur. These were some of the thoughts triggered off in Charles's mind as he lay in his hammock or sat on deck reading Lyell's *Principles*. Lyell himself had not so much as hinted that his reasoning could be applied to the plant and animal world.

Charles had one or two outstanding experiences during the voyage which, as an enthusiastic new Uniformitarian, set him thinking about natural causes and evolutions. Firstly, he soon discovered that the substratum of the pampas was one colossal tomb of strange monsters. He wrote to his sister Catherine from East Falkland Island in April 1834 with the news that he had found some perfect bones of what he believed to be a mastodon or elephant: 'There is nothing like geology; the pleasure of the first day's partridge shooting or first day's hunting cannot be compared to finding a fine group of fossil bones, which tell their story of former times with almost a living tongue.'

At Bahia Blanca, on the coast south of Buenos Aires, Charles came across a tomb of giants from earlier ages. He dug out of the beach, within an area of two hundred yards, the remains of nine large quadrupeds. They included a Megatherium – a giant sloth, a skeleton of which, fifty years earlier, had been found in the Argentine and sent to Madrid; a Megalonyx – similar to the Megatherium; a Scelidotherium – the size of a rhinoceros, with a head like that of an armadillo; a Toxodon – as large as an elephant, but related to rats and mice and other gnawers; a Mylodon – an extinct elephant, later named 'Mylodon darwinii'. As Charles surveyed his macabre handiwork in this palaeontological cemetery, he began to wonder why these extinct species of animals should bear so strong a resemblance to certain living American animals. Littered around him were the relics of bygone sloths, armadillos and giant llamas. But he also saw on his land expeditions from the *Beagle* live sloths, armadillos and llamas – smaller but not all that different

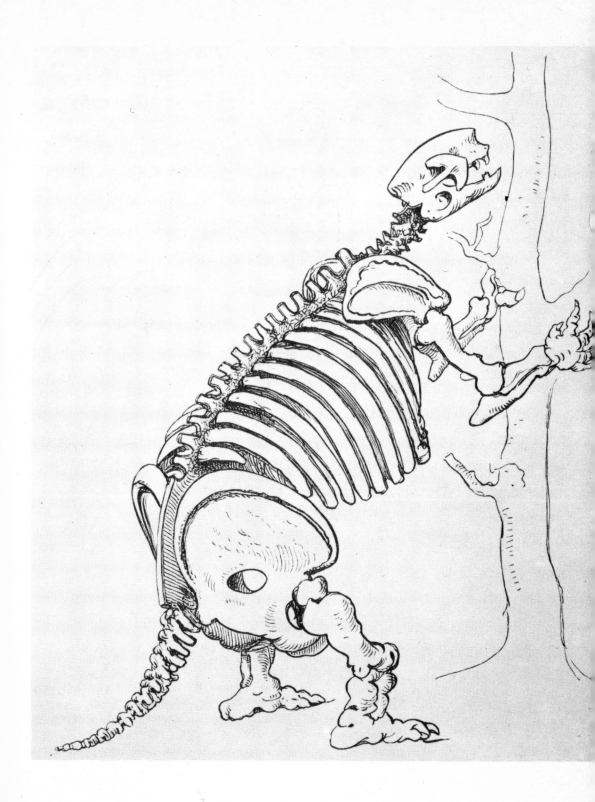

from their prehistoric counterparts. 'This wonderful relationship in the same continent between the dead and the living will, I do not doubt, hereafter throw more light on the appearance of organic beings on earth and their disappearance from it.'

Cuvier would have insisted that this relationship between the living and the dead was quite fortuitous. God had been pleased to create the ancient Megatheria and Glyptodons; in one of his destructive moods he had swept them all away, but later restored the empty land with today's sloths and llamas. Lyell's *Principles* were doing their work, and Charles thought it more likely that the old animal population had not died out but had slowly turned into the species which today inhabit South America. Although some of the more grotesque giants might have disappeared, the golden thread of life had never been entirely broken. Such a theory seemed to Charles more simple and natural than the pointless and arbitrary brutality of these periodic orgies of divine destruction.

Charles later looked back at these moments on the pampas, as he stood in this palaeontological graveyard, as part of his evolutionary awakening. He was not, as yet, beset with doubts about God – only with doubts about the ancient armadillo – and he was not disposed to deny the truths of the Bible. FitzRoy, moreover, was heading towards a fanatical fundamentalism and convinced of the factual accuracy of every Biblical statement. Knowing what FitzRoy was like when contradicted, Charles was unlikely to press his incipient evolutionary ideas too strongly. There were already quite enough opportunities for argument between FitzRoy, the High Tory, and Charles, the humanitarian Liberal. It was FitzRoy's fervent hope that the findings of the naturalist he had engaged for the expedition would endorse traditional geological and biological beliefs. He realised only much later how dangerous and subversive a choice he had made.

It is possible that Fitzroy's bigoted and blinkered views on natural phenomena encouraged Charles to be more open-minded, but also that Charles's admiration for this strange man might have caused him to hold back the development of his evolutionary views. Be that as it may, the main reaction of FitzRoy and his crew to Charles's finds were practical. Wickham, the First Lieutenant who was responsible for tidiness on board, cursed the 'Fly-Catcher' or 'Philosopher', as Charles was called by the crew, for the 'damned beastly bedevilment' of the litter of his specimens: 'If I were skipper, I would soon have you and all your damned mess out of the place.' Charles, however, wrote to his father saying that Wickham, who later became Governor of Queensland, was 'a glorious fellow'. FitzRoy later spoke of 'our smiles at the apparent rubbish he frequently brought on board'. All this 'rubbish' Charles then despatched to Henslow; the Megatherium head went by brig to Liverpool. Parcels were sent off to Henslow thick and fast – bones, skins, insects, seeds. Some of the fossil bones he had sent Henslow had excited much interest among palaeontologists. Charles also learned in a letter from one of his sisters that Henslow had read some of his letters to the Philosophical Society of Cambridge and that Sedgwick had called on his father and said that he deserved a place among the leading men of science:

After reading this letter, I clambered over the mountains of Ascension with a bounding step and made the volcanic rocks resound under my geological hammer. All this shows how ambitious I was; but I think that

Icebergs in the Strait of Magellan. Darwin would have seen these when the *Beagle* rounded Cape Horn.

FUEGIA BASKET. 1833.

JEMMY'S WIFE. 1833.

JEMMY IN 1834.

JEMMY BUTTON IN 1833.

YORK MINSTER IN 1832.

YORK IN 1833.

FUEGIANS.

I can say with truth that in after years, though I cared in the highest degree for the approbation of such men as Lyell and Hooker, who were my friends, I did not care much about the general public. I do not mean to say that a favourable review on a large scale of my books did not please me greatly, but the pleasure was a fleeting one, and I am sure that I have never turned one inch out of my course to gain fame.

Another outstanding experience which turned Charles's thoughts towards evolution was the *Beagle*'s visit to the Galapagos Islands on the homeward journey. On the way the *Beagle* rounded Cape Horn. FitzRoy had on an earlier voyage taken four Fuegians aboard; three were hostages for a stolen whale-boat and a fourth had been bought from his parents for a button: hence his name of Button! FitzRoy then had the idea of 'the various advantages which might result to them and their countrymen, as well as to us, by taking them to England, educating them there as far as might be practicable, and then bringing them back to Tierra del Fuego'. He carried out this plan; one of the Fuegians died of smallpox after arriving in England; the others survived and met the King and Queen.

Well-meaning efforts to civilize natives generally come to nothing. This Fuegian experiment was no exception, and FitzRoy was anxious to return the three surviving Fuegians to their native shores. Charles did not conceal his distaste for Fuegians in general, whom he called 'miserable savages'. Button had told him that the Fuegians were cannibals and in winter ate their women. He certainly noticed that women were easily outnumbered by the men. A Fuegian boy was asked, 'Why no eat dogs?' and the boy answered 'Dog catch otter – woman good for nothing: man very hungry.' The women were first smothered and then cooked. Charles commented indignantly: 'Was anything so atrocious heard of, to work them like slaves to procure food in the summer, and in winter to eat them?'

It was in September 1835 that the *Beagle* cast anchor among the islands of the Galapagos Archipelago. They are a group of oceanic craters, off the coast of Ecuador, that have forced their way up through the ocean and developed a limited fauna and flora. In these weird, deserted islands, Charles was once again assailed by doubts about the stability of species: 'Here, both in space and time, we seem to be brought somewhat near to that great fact – that mystery of mysteries – the first appearance of new beings on this earth.'

The islands were named after the large tortoises which abound

OPPOSITE The Fuegians who accompanied FitzRoy to England and who returned with him to Tierra del Fuego, only to go to pieces after their taste of civilization.

there. Charles estimated that they weighed 200 pounds each. Next to the tortoises, the most striking things were the lizards who lived, like the tortoises, upon cacti. What particularly struck Charles was the fact that the various islands in the group all had different inhabitants. He did not at once realise the significance of this; in fact he had, rather unsystematically, been mingling the collections of two of the islands. To his pleasure, he had found twenty-five new species of birds, fifteen new species of fish and sixteen new land-shells. He was rather disappointed by the insects, although he discovered several new genera among the twenty-five species of beetles which he collected. He discovered 185 flowering plants, of which a hundred were new to science and indigenous to the archipelago. It was the vice-governor of the islands who told him that he could tell with certainty which island a tortoise came from:

I never dreamed that islands about 50 or 60 miles apart, and most of them in sight of each other, formed of precisely the same rocks, placed under a quite similar climate, rising to a nearly equal height, would have been differently tenanted. It is the fate of most voyagers no sooner to discover what is most interesting in any locality than they are hurried from it; but I ought, perhaps, to be thankful that I obtained sufficient materials to establish this most remarkable fact in the distribution of organic beings.

The birds, insects and plants all varied on the different islands. Charles attributed this phenomenon to the strong sea currents separating the northern and southern islands and to the almost total absence of wind, which meant that the birds, insects and seeds would not be blown about from island to island.

Charles described the Galapagos as a satellite attached to America or 'rather a group of satellites, physically similar, organically distinct, yet intimately related to each other, all related in a marked though much lesser degree, to the great American continent'. The curious thing about the Galapagos plants and animals was that the various species pointed to America, but were not wholly American; nor were they, as we have seen, exactly like each other on the various islands. How, then, were these islands populated? One explanation would be that God created special Galapagos animals and Galapagos plants; another explanation is that the animals and plants were brought by the current or the wind from the nearby American coast and that, after landing on the islands, they adapted themselves to their new surroundings, and were altered: hence both the resemblances and the differ-

94

W. Hawkins del.

ences. Such an explanation would assume that species were mutable. These were the dangerous thoughts passing through Charles's mind. It was only after he had returned to England and had carefully examined and classified the specimens which he had collected and was working on his book *The Geology of the Voyage of The Beagle*, that he realized the importance of his collection.

From the Galapagos Islands the *Beagle* sailed to Tahiti and then to Australia and New Zealand, reaching Keeling Island in April 1836. Here he found vast beds of coral growing in every direction and it was here that he formed his famous theories of the nature and origin of coral reefs. The three classes of coral reef were later described in his book *The Structure and Distribution of Coral Reefs* (1842).

The *Beagle* sailed on from the coral islands to Mauritius and

96

Prionotus Miles: one of the many varieties of fish found near the Galapagos Islands. This one came from the shores of Chatham Island.

BELOW Finches from the different Galapagos Islands – they could be distinguished by the size of their beaks.

Amblyrynchus Demarlii, the land iguana, was brightly coloured, sometimes four feet long, and fed upon cactus trees.

thence to St Helena and Bahia, where they had originally landed in February 1832. They had then completed the chronometrical measurement of the world. On the way up the coast, the ship stopped at Pernambuco. In his note-book Charles wrote: 'I thank God I shall never again visit a slave-country. To this day, if I hear a scream, it recalls with painful vividness my feelings, when, passing a house near Pernambuco, I heard the most pitiable moans, and could not but suspect some poor slave was being tortured.'

Streets in Sydney, another port of call in the *Beagle's* voyage.

4 Marital Bliss and Medical Mystery

IN HIS OLD AGE, Charles described the two years and three months from his return to England on 2 October 1836 to his marriage on 29 January 1839 as the most active he had ever spent, with precious time lost through occasional periods of ill health. 'A man who dares to waste one hour of time', he said, 'has not discovered the value of life.'

After landing at Falmouth, he made straight for Shrewsbury. He found his father and sisters well and cheerful. After his family, he was most anxious to see the Wedgwoods at Maer, Henslow at Cambridge and his new hero Lyell. The first thing he did was to write a grateful and affectionate letter to FitzRoy, assuring him that he would keep an eye on the dangerous radicalism of his family: 'I must tell you for the honour and glory of my family that my father has a large engraving of King George IV put up in his sitting-room.' To his uncle, Josiah Wedgwood, he wrote,

> My head is quite confused with so much delight, but I cannot allow my sister to tell you first how happy I am to see all my dear friends again ... I am most anxious once again to see Maer, and all its inhabitants, so that in the course of two or three weeks, I hope in person to thank you, as being my First Lord of the Admiralty.

By this, Charles was referring to the fact that it was only his uncle's intervention which had given him the great opportunity of his life.

Charles also wrote Henslow saying that he intended to visit him at once in Cambridge on his way to London, where the *Beagle* staff were being paid off. He confessed that he was 'in the clouds, and neither know what to do or where to go'. His main worry was finding someone to help him describe the mineralogical character of his geological specimens: 'My dear Henslow, I do long to see you; you have been the kindest friend to me that ever man possessed. I can write no more, for I am giddy with joy and confusion.' Charles's exquisite sensation of delight at being home again could not, as is always the case, last long. At Greenwich he started, with a sinking heart, to unpack his vast collection of specimens from the *Beagle*. He was at his wit's end to find any professional naturalist who would examine them for him and he soon realized that he would have to do most of the work himself. He was overwhelmed by the immensity of the task and doubted whether he possessed the necessary ability and intellectual and physical stamina.

Gradually, with the encouragement of Lyell and other distinguished naturalists, Charles's confidence returned. He found that he was, at the age of twenty-eight, one of the best-equipped and

PREVIOUS PAGES Marcaw Cottage in Gower Street: Darwin's home in the early days of his married life.

OPPOSITE Samuel Lawrence's portrait of Darwin in 1853.

Lyell, who helped Darwin in the immense task of classifying the specimens he had brought home from his journey round the world.

most versatile naturalists of the day. If the worst came to the worst, he could undertake single-handed the examination and classification of his collection. This turned out not to be necessary. He found different experts for certain jobs – the dissection of animals in spirits; the examination of corallines; the classification of shells; the arrangement of birds and fishes. This left Charles with the rocks and minerals. He decided to spend the next three months in Cambridge working on them. He realized that he would, after that, have to move to 'dirty, odious London' in order to complete his geological work and push on with zoology. The only extinct South American mammals which had, at this time, been described were the Mastodon and Megatherium. Charles's speci-

John Stevens Henslow, the
Cambridge professor of
botany, who encouraged
Darwin's interest in
natural history.

mens included the Toxodon, Scelidotherium and the remains of the
Mylodon, Glossotherium and Macrancheria. These remains
Charles had dug up with his own hands and they provided one of
the chief starting-points for his speculations on the origin of
species. A few months later he wrote in his pocket book, 'In July
[1837] opened first note-book on Transmutation of Species. Had
been greatly struck from about the month of previous March on
character of South American fossils, and species on Galapagos
Archipelago. These facts (especially latter), origin of all my
views.'

In March 1837 he took lodgings in Great Marlborough Street in
London and remained there until he married. During these two

107

Patagonian natives in their *toldo* (tent).

years, he finished his *Journal of Researches*, the first issue of which had formed the third volume of FitzRoy's set; he arranged for the publication of *The Zoology of the Voyage of the Beagle* and began preparing his own *Geology of the Voyage of the Beagle*. Earlier, Henslow had published, without Charles's knowledge, under the title *Letters on Geology*, some extracts of letters which Charles had written him during the *Beagle* voyage. In July, Charles opened his first notebook for facts in relation to the *Origin of Species*, 'about

108

which I had long reflected, and never ceased working on for the next 20 years'.

During this time, Charles read one or two papers before the Geological Society at the Royal Academy – on coral formation and on the pampas; on earthworms; on volcanic phenomena and the formation of mountain chains and on the 'Rhea Americanus'. Thanks largely to the little book which Henslow had had published without his knowledge, and to the comparative stir created

An impression by FitzRoy of Fuegians trading with Patagonians in Zapallos.

OPPOSITE The bay of San Carlos, the capital of the island of Chiloe: one of Martens's illustrations.

by the many undescribed species which he had brought back with him, Charles was offered the post of secretary to the Geological Society. He accepted with reluctance because of the extra work which it might entail. It was now that the constant ill-health, from which he suffered after his marriage, became apparent. This, and his growing passion for scientific work for its own sake, were to determine the character of the secluded life he was to lead until his death. He began to have palpitations of the heart, which he had also suffered at Plymouth during those two agonizing months of waiting for the *Beagle* to set sail.

During his two years as a bachelor in London, Charles went out in society. He saw a lot of Lyell, who was handsome, easy-going and sociable; he saw the Carlyles at the house of his brother Erasmus and he met many leading men of the time at the Athenaeum Club. Apart from his scientific work, he did some general reading – either metaphysical books, which he found heavy-going, or poetry; the poets he preferred were Coleridge, Wordsworth and Milton, whose *Paradise Lost* had been his constant companion

110

on the *Beagle*. Yet Charles felt that there was something lacking in his life; he hated London and pined both for Shrewsbury and for Maer:

My God, it is intolerable to think of spending one's whole life like a neuter bee living all one's days solitarily in smoky, dirty London. Only picture to yourself a nice soft wife on a sofa, with good fire and books and music perhaps – compare this vision with the dingy reality of Gt. Marboro' St. ... Marry, Marry, Marry! Q.E.D.

A volcano in the Cordilleras. Darwin witnessed a similar one when in Chiloe, and later saw the ruins of Concepcion in Chile.

These requirements of a wife seemed to point to Emma Wedgwood, his attractive, cheerful, lovable first cousin. Emma was pretty, with abundant rich brown hair, grey eyes and a fresh complexion, a firm chin, a high forehead and a straight nose. She was of medium height, with well-formed shoulders and pretty arms and hands. Her nickname was 'little Miss Slip-Slop', on account of her general disorderliness. Charles said that he decided, when marrying her, to give up his natural taste for tidiness, so that he would not be annoyed by her lack of interest in such matters. She was encouraged by her parents to read and think for herself and she became, by any standards, a well-educated woman. She knew French, Italian and German; Charles, who claimed not to know a word of any foreign language, used her for translating. Her character was firm, calm and clear; everything she undertook she did well – she was a beautiful needlewoman and a good archer. She rode, danced and skated. Her chief accomplishment was music. She played delightfully on the piano until the very end of her life, although she said that she had never practised for more than an hour a day. She had a crisp and fine touch and always played with intelligence and simplicity. She would endure nothing sentimental and preferred to take slow movements *'allegro'*. Chopin gave her a few lessons. Although she was calm about music, she once lost her self-control when Clara Novello, the operatic prima-donna, sang 'God Save The Queen' at the opening of the Crystal Palace. This was towards the end of her great career, but her singing on that day was, according to the newspapers, grander than ever before and 'heard to remote corners of the building'. Emma broke down and sobbed audibly. Her daughter spoke of the scene as 'extraordinarily impressive – the standing crowd, the Queen and Prince Albert present, and the wonderful volume of the rich soprano voice, sustained and round and full, filling the enormous building'.

It was in the summer of 1838 that Charles decided to ask Emma to be his wife. They were both thirty years of age. He was not, according to his daughter, at all hopeful, 'for he had the strange idea that his delightful face, so full of power and sweetness, was repellently plain'. However, he had the courage to put his fate to her in the library at Maer and was at once accepted. The news gave unalloyed pleasure to all members of both families. Robert wrote to Josiah, 'Emma having accepted Charles gives me as great pleasure as Jos having married Caroline, and I cannot say more.' Jos was the eldest son of Josiah Wedgwood and had his father's

reserved and formal manner, but was even more diffident; his mother had for several years been doing her best to promote a match between him and Caroline Darwin, Charles's eldest sister. But nothing happened. At last, in 1837, the year Queen Victoria came to the throne, they married; he was forty-two and she was thirty-seven. There is no mention of either event in the Maer and Shrewsbury papers.

Josiah was equally pleased with Emma's engagement to Charles and he proposed to allow her £400 a year, 'as long as my income will supply it, which I have no reason for thinking will not be as long as I live'. Emma herself had this to say about Charles:

> He is the most open transparent man I ever saw, and every word expresses his real thoughts. He is particularly affectionate and very nice to his father and sisters, and perfectly sweet-tempered, and possesses some minor qualities that add particularly to one's happiness, such as not being fastidious, and being humane to animals.

As for Charles, he wrote to Lyell with the news and explaining how they were 'connected by manifold ties, besides on my part, by the most sincere love and hearty gratitude to her for accepting such a one as myself'.

Charles and Emma were married on 29 January 1839 in Maer Church. It was a quiet wedding and they afterwards went to their new furnished house in Upper Gower Street. Charles called their new home 'Marcaw Cottage' because of the colour of the 'furnishing'. It was a typical three-storeyed, middle-class house, dark and narrow, with a kitchen and scullery in the semi-basement.

A few days before their wedding, Charles wrote Emma an interesting letter about himself:

> I was thinking this morning how it came that I, who am fond of talking and scarcely ever out of spirits, should so entirely rest my notion of happiness on quietness and a good deal of solitude. But I believe the explanation is very simple, and I mention it because it will give you hope that I shall gradually grow less of a brute. It is that during the five years of my voyage (and indeed I may add these last two), which from the active manner in which they have been passed, may be said to be the commencement of my real life, the whole of my pleasure was derived from what passed in my mind while admiring views by myself, travelling across the wild deserts or glorious forests, or pacing the deck of the poor little *Beagle* at night. Excuse this much egotism; I give it you because I think you will humanize me, and soon teach me there is greater happiness than building theories and accumulating facts in silence and solitude.

116

This letter reads like a *cri de coeur* to Emma to rescue him from the dreaded plight of the intellectual – the retreat from spontaneity. It reminds us of Coleridge's anguished cry in his *Dejection: an Ode:* 'I see, not feel how beautiful they are!' Charles could no longer recapture the carefree moods of his Cambridge days, 'the most joyful in my happy life; for I was then in excellent health and almost always in high spirits'. The last seven years, starting with the *Beagle* voyage, had completely changed his earlier mental habits; the intellectual excitement and discipline of careful observation and the building of theories had taken possession of his mind. Charles, while preserving his engaging affability and friendliness, had become a person obsessed.

Wordsworth, another of Charles's favourite poets, had expressed, in his *Ode on the Intimations of Immortality*, the anguish of beholding, but not inwardly experiencing, the marvellous works of Nature. We know, from his letters and journal, that Charles was deeply affected by the splendour of the 'scenic wonders' which crowded in upon his senses during the *Beagle* voyage; his scientific awakening may have turned them into phenomena to be analysed and dissected, to form the basis of general laws. Although conscious of the importance of every minute of the day in his scientific quest for arriving at the origin of life on earth, he was never in a hurry; a fine example of his inexhaustible patience is illustrated by an experiment described in his *Vegetable Mould and Earth-worms*, in which a layer of chalk was laid upon a patch of ground in 1842 and the result quietly waited for until 1871.

However, as Charles himself bitterly lamented, his absorption in science led steadily, after his marriage, to the atrophy of his artistic sensibility, which had never been very marked. He no longer much appreciated good pictures, poetry and music, and the plays of Shakespeare he found intolerably dull!

The collapse of Charles's health and his sudden ageing date from his marriage. He went bald; he suffered from eczema, boils, fainting fits, headaches, trembling of the hands, tooth and gum problems, arthritis, catarrh, palpitations, nausea, vomiting, flatulence, insomnia and chronic exhaustion! Poor Emma must have wondered what she had done to deserve this. One explanation offered by an American psychiatrist was that Charles 'slew the Heavenly Father in the realm of natural history' and that his punishment was to be forty years of severe and crippling neurotic suffering!

117

'Felis Pajeros', a pampas cat found at Santa Cruz, Patagonia.

Ill-health is a recurrent theme of Charles's letters from the date of his marriage until his death. When offered the secretaryship of the Geological Society, he wrote to Henslow that he doubted 'how far my health will stand the confinement of what I have to do, without any additional work'. His doctor had advised him to give up writing and proof correcting for several weeks: 'Of late, anything which flurries me completely knocks me up afterwards, and brings on a violent palpitation of the heart.' Although Charles's many doctors never ventured to come to any definite conclusions as to the causes of his long bouts of illness, their hesitancy has been amply made up for by modern medical writers and psychiatrists. Speculative and dogmatic articles on the nature of his illness have proliferated in recent years and, since we shall never know its cause, there is no reason to suppose that the last word has been said.

Darwin, as we shall henceforward call Charles, has been chosen as a convenient and, because of his fame, dramatic example of the lack of emotional frankness, morbidity, psychological ignorance and even hypocrisy which, people like to think, represent 'the other side' of the formidable Victorian era. Hence the aggressive satisfaction of contemporary prattle about our 'emancipation' from Victorian sexual and social prejudices. Darwin's ill-health is, nevertheless, an interesting subject. If real, it demonstrated his fortitude and will-power; if imagined, it adds a touch of complexity to a character whose transparent truthfulness and simplicity attracted everyone who came into contact with him.

Some of the psychological theories about his health, which have been elaborated in the course of this century, can take their place in an anthology of the absurdities of psychoanalytical literature. Darwin's health has, however, been the subject of Freudian analytical techniques and all the theories which have been put forward, whether true or untrue, have had a salutary humanizing effect. They have done no harm to the reputation of the melancholy Victorian recluse. Darwin, who took so great an interest in his symptoms, would have willingly agreed to their examination by the new system of psychoanalysis whose founder, Freud, was as great an intellectual force in the twentieth century as Darwin had been in the nineteenth. Moreover, in the eyes of the world, they were both guilty of similar offences – Darwin had banished God from nature and Freud had banished Him from the soul.

Another feature of Darwin, which the psychoanalysts have often linked to his illness, was his extraordinary diffidence. He had what amounted to a pathological reluctance to publish his ideas on the sticky subject of evolution. This has led to a theory that his illness and diffidence were both neurotic symptoms springing from an unconscious conflict with Robert Darwin; in this way, he expressed the hatred, aggression and resentment which he felt towards his tyrannical father, which he covered up by frequent and effusive expressions of love and reverence. Darwin's feelings of guilt about the subject are clearly shown in a letter to Hooker in which he said that his growing belief that species were not immutable was 'like confessing a murder'. Robert Darwin, however, may well have believed in evolution, since he took over most of his father's ideas, and this could have been one of the subconscious sources of his own son's beliefs.

Another theory is that Darwin was neither clever nor quick-witted, that he needed more time than most people to think out his theories. His obsessive desire to work and achieve something was prompted by hatred and resentment of his father, who had called him an idler and good-for-nothing during his youth. He could

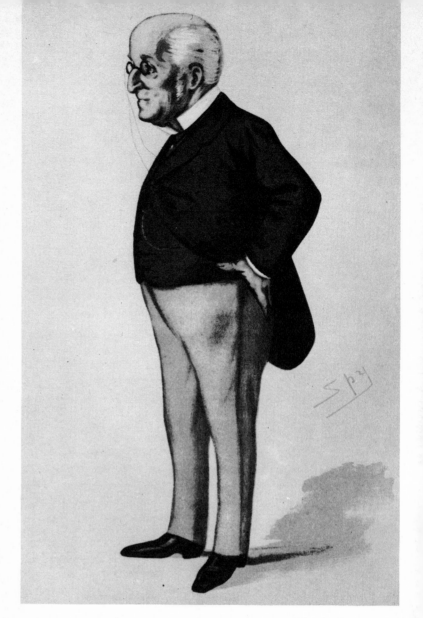

Dr James Manby Gully, whom Darwin consulted several times and whose water cure he used. Gully was also said to have had a hand in the murder of his lover's husband.

OPPOSITE Sir Andrew Clark, Darwin's Scottish physician.

achieve anything only by exchanging the distractions of London for the solitude of the country. This view was, at least partially, endorsed by Darwin when he said, 'Even ill-health, though it has annihilated several years of my life, has saved me from the distraction of society and amusement.'

There has been, needless to say, a sexual explanation of Darwin's illness. It was, the theory goes, a neurotic manifestation of a conflict between a sense of duty to his father and a sexual attachment to his mother, who died when he was eight. The titles of his books also show his intense preoccupation with sexual matters;

120

for example, *Cross and self-fertilisation,* and *Fertilisation of Orchids*.

The emphasis has, in recent years, shifted from pure psychogenic (springing from the mind) causes towards more straightforward medical ones, some of which are, in their way, equally fanciful and inventive. The most readily accepted diagnosis appears now to be that Darwin had a genuine illness, aggravated by his hypochondria. The illness was probably Chagas's Disease, named after the Brazilian botanist who first defined it. Darwin may have caught it in March 1865 in the Argentine when he was attacked by the Benchuca, the huge, blood-sucking bug of the pampas, known as 'Triatoma infestans'. This bug is the carrier of the trypanosoma, the micro-organism which causes the disease. The symptoms of Chagas's Disease correspond perfectly with Darwin's medical history from the time when he landed in England from the *Beagle* until his death. The trypanosoma invades the heart muscles of its victim, leaving him very tired; it also invades other parts of the body, causing lassitude, gastro-intestinal discomfort and heart trouble, of which Darwin died.

Darwin was no better than his doctors at diagnosing his illness. Since his whole intellectual life consisted of collecting facts, it must have been embarrassing for him to have, in the case of his bad state of health, little worthwhile evidence to adduce. He had, in his youth, been rather proud of his diagnostic ability when he helped his father in Shrewsbury: 'I noted down as full an account as I could of the cases with all the symptoms, and read them aloud to my father, who suggested further enquiries, and advised what medicine to give, which I made up myself. At one time I had at least half a dozen patients, and I felt a keen interest in the work.'

To make matters worse, Darwin looked quite well; his friends commented on his ruddy, out-of-door complexion, although he preferred to describe it as 'rather sallow'. It is now thought that his ruddy looks were caused by chronic arsenic poisoning! Darwin had taken arsenic at Cambridge as a cure for eczema of the hands and mouth. He had wanted, naturally enough, to get rid of his eczema before joining the *Beagle*. Some psychiatrists, however, have suggested that the real 'reason' was his homosexual attachment to the handsome Captain FitzRoy. It was not uncommon to prescribe arsenic in those days, although his father did not approve of the practice. Darwin went on to suffer throughout his life from the occasional fierce attack of eczema. Hooker spoke of his 'violent eczema in the head, during which time he was hardly recognizable'. This is not an attractive picture of Darwin. He was always grateful to Hooker for taking his illness seriously: 'Every one tells me that I look quite blooming and beautiful; and most think I am shamming, but you have never been one of these.'

Darwin's children, at least, took his illness as seriously as he did himself. His son and collaborator, Francis Darwin, was certain that his sufferings were genuine:

He bore his illness with such uncomplaining patience, that even his children can hardly, I believe, realise the extent of his habitual suffering. ... No one indeed, except my mother, knows the full amount of the suffering he endured, or the full amount of his wonderful patience. For all the latter years of his life she never left him for a night; and her days were so planned that all his resting hours might be shared with her. She shielded him from every avoidable annoyance, and omitted nothing that might save him trouble, or prevent him becoming overtired, or that might alleviate the many discomforts of his ill-health ... it is a principal feature of his life, that for nearly 40 years he never knew for one day the health of ordinary men, and that thus his life was one long struggle against the weariness and strain of sickness.

If Darwin's kindness and gentleness to his children and friends was, as one or two psychiatrists have suggested, merely a mask to cover up the tyrannical and blackmailing uses to which he put his illness, he was certainly very successful.

5 Darwin at Home

ABOVE Julia Wedgwood's painting of Down House seen from the back garden.

LEFT George Richmond's portraits of Darwin and his wife.

PREVIOUS PAGES (124–5) Down House, Kent, where
Darwin spent forty years of his life and wrote his
most important books.

DARWIN AND HIS WIFE lived at Upper Gower Street from their marriage on 29 January 1839 until they moved to their new house in Kent on 14 September 1842. Emma quickly became the ideal sick-nurse and Darwin the ideal patient. In the early days of his marriage, he still felt strong enough to go into general society; he attended meetings of scientific societies and saw a certain amount of his friends Lyell and Henslow. They went to occasional dinner-parties, at one of which he met his old idol Alexander von Humboldt, who always remained for him 'the greatest scientific traveller who ever lived'. These outings proved to be too much for him and the Darwins decided to move to the country as soon as they could find somewhere suitable. 'We are living a life of extreme quietness. ... We have given up all parties, for they agree with neither of us.' It is hard to believe that the cheerful and gregarious Emma really shared these sentiments; she decided, presumably, to acquiesce in them for her husband's sake.

In December 1839 their first child, William, was born. Darwin was very proud of him and a few months later wrote, 'He is so charming that I cannot pretend to any modesty. I defy anyone to flatter us on our baby, for I defy anyone to say anything in its praise of which we are not fully conscious. ... I had not the smallest conception that there was so much in a five-month baby.' In 1877, he published a short paper, *A biographical sketch of an infant,* based on the minute observation which he had recorded in a diary on the first few months of his child's life, nearly forty years earlier. His passion for fact-finding and theorizing had, as the diary shows, got a firm hold on him and his mind was becoming what he called 'a kind of machine for grinding general laws out of large collections of facts'.

This sketch, of which he later made use in *The expression of the emotions in man and animals* (1872), has been highly praised by modern child neurologists who claim that, in it, Darwin conquered 'most of developmental psychology in a single sweep'. In this essay the two enthusiasms of his life – science and his family – were neatly blended. He studied the early movements and expressions of his son with the same care as those of an earth-worm:

During the first seven days various reflex actions, namely sneezing, hiccuping, yawning, stretching and, of course, sucking and screaming, were well performed by my infant. On the seventh day, I touched the naked sole of his foot with a bit of paper, and he jerked it away, curling at the same time his toes, like a much older child when tickled. The perfection of these reflex movements shows that the extreme imperfection of

Two of Wood's drawings for Darwin's *Expression of the Emotions in Man and Animals*: 'Chimpanzee disappointed and sulky' *(right)*; 'Cat terrified at a dog' *(opposite)*.

the voluntary ones is not due to the state of the muscles or of the co-ordinating centres, but to that of the seat of the will.

Darwin recorded the different impressions of each of his infant's emotions and then went on, characteristically, to form conclusions. Fear, for example:

This feeling is probably one of the earliest which is experienced by infants, as shown by their starting at any sudden sound when only a few weeks old, followed by crying. Before the present one was $4\frac{1}{2}$ months old, I had been accustomed to make close to him many strange and loud noises, which were all taken as excellent jokes, but at this period I one day made a loud snoring noise which I had never done before; he instantly looked grave and then burst out crying. Two or three days afterwards, I made through forgetfulness the same noise with the same result. About the same time (viz., on the 137th day) I approached with my back towards him and then stood motionless. He looked very grave and much surprised, and would soon have cried, had I not turned round;

130

then his face instantly relaxed into a smile. It is well known how intensely older children suffer from vague and undefined fears, as from the dark, or in passing an obscure corner in a large hall, etc. I may give as an instance that I took the child in question, when $2\frac{1}{2}$ years old, to the Zoological Gardens, and he enjoyed looking at the animals which were like those that he knew, such as deer, antelopes, etc., and all the birds, even the ostriches, but was much alarmed at the various larger animals in cages. He often said afterwards that he wished to go again, but not to see 'beasts in houses'; and we could in no manner account for this fear. May we not suspect that the vague but very real fears of children, which are quite independent of experience, are the inherited effects of real dangers and abject superstitions during ancient savage times? It is quite conformable with what we know of the transmission of formerly well-developed characters, that they should appear at an early period of life and then disappear.

Darwin's principal achievement during his early married years in London was the completion of his book on coral reefs. 'This book, though a small one, cost me 20 months of hard work, as I had to read every work on the Islands of the Pacific and to consult many charts. It was thought highly of by scientific men, and the theory therein given is, I think, now well established.' What Darwin then said holds good today; his theory has stood triumphantly the test of time and become incorporated in standard geological text-books. He called this the only one of his works to be strongly deductive in character, that is, using a theory as a starting point, since he had elaborated the whole theory on the west coast of South America before he had seen a single coral reef! His theory explains both why coral reefs appear where they do and also why they do not appear in places where one might expect to find them. He thus summed up his studies of coral reefs:

When the two great types of structure, namely barrier-reefs and atolls on the one hand, and fringing reefs on the other, are laid down on a map, they offer a grand and harmonious picture of the movements which the crust of the earth has undergone within a later period. We see these vast areas rising, with volcanic matter every now and then bursting forth. We see other wide spaces sinking without any volcanic outbursts; and we may feel sure that the movement has been so slow as to allow the corals to grow up to the surface, and so widely extended as to have buried over the broad face of the oceans every one of those mountains, above which the atolls now stand like monuments, marking the place of their burial.

Lyell heard Darwin's views on the formation of coral-reefs soon after the *Beagle*'s return; although they spelled the end of his own cherished volcanic crater theory, he was very happy to be in-

structed by his pupil: 'Lyell, on receiving from the lips of its
author a sketch of the new theory, was so overcome with delight
that he danced about and threw himself into the wildest contor-
tions, as was his manner when excessively pleased.'

In September 1842 the Darwins left London for their new house
in the village of Downe in Kent. We know, by now, only too well
the reasons which induced them to move to the country. They had
been searching fruitlessly, in Surrey and elsewhere, for a house
which would be secluded, in pleasant country and within easy

Sir Francis Galton, scientist
and cousin of Darwin, painted
by C. W. Furse. His most
notable achievements were in
the field of eugenics.

133

William Henry Fitton,
geologist and physician, who
was a friend of Darwin from
about 1839.

access of London. Down House met, more or less, these requirements and Robert Darwin advanced the money, £2,020, to buy it.
Neither Darwin nor his wife was much enamoured of their new
home, which they had chosen mainly out of weariness of house-
hunting. They decided that its attractive points outweighed its
disadvantages. The house, which today belongs to the Royal
College of Surgeons, is very much as it was when Darwin lived
there. It stands a quarter of a mile from the village on a narrow,
winding lane off the Westerham road. The village is today spelled
'Downe', with an 'e', a spelling of which the Darwins strongly
disapproved. It is in an angle between two roads, one leading to

134

Robert Brown was the naturalist on the Flinders expedition and a pioneer in the study of fossil plant anatomy. He later became librarian to the Linnean Society.

Tunbridge and the other to Westerham and Edenbridge. It had then three or four hundred inhabitants and consisted of a few rows of cottages which met in front of a little flint-built church. The features of the country are its wide, rolling downs overlooked by 'shaws', straggling strips of wood on steep chalky hills. The smugglers and their strings of pack-horses used to make their way to Downe along the narrow, tortuous lanes.

Darwin intended to make frequent visits to London: 'I hope by going up to town for a night every fortnight or three weeks, to keep up my communication with scientific men and my own zeal, and so not to turn into a complete Kentish hog.' Although he did

135

Darwin's comfortable and
cluttered 'New Study' at
Down House.

137

this for a few years, until his health put a stop to it, he never liked those ten-mile drives to Croydon or Sydenham – the nearest stations – with an old gardener who acted as coachman and drove, with extreme slowness and caution, up and down the many hills.

Darwin described the house as 'ugly, looks neither old nor new'. He did not dislike the country as much as Emma, who found it 'desolate': 'I think all chalk countries do, but I am used to Cambridgeshire, which is ten times worse.' He was taken by the rusticity of the surroundings: 'The charm of the place to me is that almost every field is intersected (as alas is ours) by one or more foot-paths. I never saw so many walks in any other county. The country is extraordinarily rural and quiet with narrow lanes and high hedges and hardly any ruts. It is really surprising to think that London is only 16 miles off.'

Shortly after Darwin and his family moved in, work was started to make the house more secluded, attractive and larger. A squarish Georgian three-storeyed brick building, it looked not unlike The Mount, his father's house in Shrewsbury. The lane, which divided Down House from its neighbour, was lowered two feet; the house was covered with stucco, and a large bow was built on the garden front, covering three storeys. This bow was covered with a wooden frame and gradually became an agreeable tangle of creepers. At a later stage, the drawing-room and its verandah, opening into the garden, were added.

Eighteen acres of land went with the house. Most of this was a field, out of which Darwin took a few strips to improve the garden. He made banks and mounds around the lawn and planted them with evergreens; he also made a new vegetable garden. The most famous feature of Down is what has come to be known as Darwin's 'Sand-Walk'. At the far south of the field, he planted a strip, about three hundred yards long, of limes, maples, elms, oaks, and birches, which were varied with flowering shrubs. He encircled this with a path, which he covered with sand from a nearby sand-pit. It became Darwin's fixed habit to take his daily exercise in the sand-walk, generally between finishing his morning's work in his study and his return for lunch at one o'clock. He kept a pile of flints by the side of this circular path and kicked one off each time he made a complete round.

Darwin was thirty-three when he moved to Down. He was to live there until he died, forty years later. In a letter to FitzRoy he writes, 'My life goes on like clockwork, and I am fixed on the spot where I shall end it.' The routine of his life was, from now

138

Darwin, 'the shoulders of an Atlas supporting a world of thoughts', gave a warm welcome to his visitors at Down.

onwards, broken only by an occasional visit to a health resort, to London or to Shrewsbury. There are no further 'phases' of his life to record. He had already acquired the characteristics of age – studiousness, reflective habits, preoccupation with health, desire for seclusion, disenchantment with worldly affairs and a narrowing of his intellectual interests. Darwin said of himself at this time, 'My chief enjoyment and sole employment throughout life has been scientific work, and the excitement from such work makes me for the time forget, or drives quite away, my daily discomfort. I have therefore nothing to record during the rest of my life, except the publication of my several books.' Neither did his character,

Sir John Lubbock, friend and neighbour of the Darwins.

over the years, betray the usual signs of age, such as increasing mellowness or crustiness. The impressions of visitors to Down are invariably constant – the sweetness of Darwin's disposition, his modesty and transparent truthfulness, his love of his children are the recurrent themes. In later years, when he was famous and venerable, a note of awe and of astonishment enters into these descriptions.

Darwin's children said that their earliest recollections of their father coincided with their latest. His son Francis said that his earliest and latest memories of his father were on the 'Sand-Walk':

He walked with a swinging action using a stick heavily shod with iron which he struck loudly against the ground, producing a rythmical click that is with all of us a very distinct remembrance. As he returned from the midday walk, often carrying the waterproof or cloak which had proved too hot, one could see that the swinging step was kept up by something of an effort. Indoors his step was often slow and laboured, and as he went upstairs in the afternoon he might be heard mounting the stairs with a heavy footfall, as if each step were an effort. When interested in his work he moved about quickly and easily enough, and often in the middle of dictating he went eagerly into the hall to get a pinch of snuff, leaving the study door open, and calling out the last word of his sentence as he went.

This description is as applicable in 1842 as in 1882.

A vivid first impression of Darwin at Down in later life is given by another of the great scientists of the nineteenth century, Ernst Haeckel, who was known as 'the Darwin of Germany'. He was twenty-five years younger than Darwin. This, the first of several visits by Haeckel to Down, took place in 1865:

In Darwin's own carriage, which he had thoughtfully sent for my convenience to the railway station, I drove one sunny morning in October through the graceful hilly landscape of Kent, that with the chequered foliage of its woods, with its stretches of purple heath, yellow broom, and evergreen oaks, was arrayed in its fairest autumnal dress. As the carriage drew up in front of Darwin's pleasant country-house, clad in a vesture of ivy and embowered in elms, there stepped out to meet me from the shady porch, overgrown with creeping plants, the great naturalist himself, a tall and venerable figure, with the shoulders of an Atlas supporting a world of thoughts, his Jupiter-like forehead highly and broadly arched, as in the case of Goethe, and deeply furrowed by the mental plough of labour; his kindly mild eyes looking forth under the shadow of prominent brows; his amiable mouth surrounded by a copious silver-white beard. The cordial, prepossessing expression of the whole face, the gentle mild voice, the slow, deliberate utterances, the natural and naive

140

train of ideas which marked his conversation, captivated my whole heart in the first hour of our meeting, just as his great work had formerly, on my first reading it, taken my whole understanding by storm. I fancied a lofty world sage out of Hellenic antiquity – a Socrates or Aristotle stood before me.

Although Darwin may have assumed, unusually early in life, the settled and peaceful habits of old age, this did not mean that his household was lacking in animation. Emma had ten children between 1839 and 1856 – six sons and four daughters. Furthermore, they made some new friends, whose visits became an essential part of life at Down. The most important event of the year 1844 was the beginning of a lifelong friendship with 'Joe' Hooker, later the great Sir Joseph Dalton Hooker of Kew. Hooker's description of Darwin, who was eight years older, in those early days at Down is naturally more earth-bound than that of Haeckel:

A more hospitable and more attractive home under every point of view could not be imagined. ... There were long walks, romps with the children on hands and knees, music that haunts me still. Darwin's own hearty manner, hollow laugh, and thorough enjoyment of home life with friends; strolls with him all together, and interviews with him one by one in his study, to discuss questions in any branch of geological or physical knowledge that we had followed; and which I at any rate always left with the feeling that I had imparted nothing and carried away more than I could stagger under.

Hooker had just returned from the Antarctic; a year or two later he left for India to study the exotic botany of the tropics. Darwin had become very attached to his new friend: 'It will be a noble voyage and journey, but I wish it was over, I shall miss you selfishly and all ways to a dreadful extent.'

Another important friendship at about this time was started with Thomas Henry Huxley, who had just returned from a surveying voyage to Australia and New Guinea in HMS *Rattlesnake*. Huxley became a familiar face at Down and Darwin's fearless and untiring protagonist when the evolutionary storm later broke: 'His mind is as quick as a flash of lightning and as sharp as a razor. He is the best talker I have ever known. He never writes and never says anything flat.' Darwin did not always approve of Huxley's relish for controversy. Huxley saw himself as 'Darwin's bulldog', his duty being to defend his friend against stupid and malicious attacks. He later had, as we shall see, plenty of opportunities to use his talents in this cause.

Darwin loved the quietness and rusticity of Down. 'It is not,

Sir Joseph Dalton Hooker, with Lyell one of Darwin's most loyal supporters, and director of Kew Gardens.

however,' he said, 'quite so retired a place as a writer in a German periodical makes it, who says that my house can be approached only by a muletrack!'

It is remarkable that he, with his constant suffering, should have shown so few, if any, signs of irascibility; had he been a Christian, his meekness and patience could be given as excellent examples of the efficacy of prayer and spiritual self-discipline. His children never remembered his speaking an angry word, yet it did not occur to them to disobey him.

I well remember [said his son Francis] one occasion when my father reproved me for a piece of carelessness; and I can still recall the feeling of depression which came over me, and the care which he took to disperse it by speaking to me soon afterwards with especial kindness. He kept his delightful, affectionate manner towards us all his life. I sometimes wonder that he could do so, with such an undemonstrative race as we are; but I hope he knew how much we delighted in his loving words and manner. How often, when a man, I have wished when my father was behind my chair, that he would pass his hand over my hair, as he used to do when I was a boy.

What was Darwin's daily routine at Down? He got up early, went for a short walk and then breakfasted alone at 7.45, after which he retired to his study. He considered the hour and a half between 8 a.m. and 9.30 to be his best working time. When the post arrived, at about 9.30, the letters were read to him as he lay on the sofa; the reading aloud included part of a novel – preferably with a pretty heroine and a happy ending. This lasted until 10.30, after which he went back to his study to work until midday. (Darwin did not have any respect for books as such. He thought nothing of breaking a book in half, if that made it easier and less tiring for him to read!) At midday, Darwin's day's work was over and he started his walk. After lunch he read the newspaper lying on the sofa in the drawing-room. Everything else was read aloud to him. Early in the afternoon, he attended to his correspondence and then rested again on the sofa smoking a cigarette, a habit he acquired among the *gauchos* in South America. At 4 o'clock he took another walk and then worked from 4.30 to 5:30. In the evening he played backgammon with his wife.

OPPOSITE Thomas Henry Huxley. He claimed that 'The *Origin* provided us with the working hypothesis we sought' and devoted much time and energy to popularizing the theory of natural selection.

145

6 The Origin of Species

L. WELLS DEL.   BUTTERWORTH & HEATH SC.

THE PRINCIPLE OF NATURAL SELECTION was Darwin's greatest discovery. He began, on his return from the *Beagle*, his famous notebooks 'for the collection of facts which bore in any way on the variation of animals and plants under domestication and in nature'. He had been struck by the efficacy of selection in creating new varieties and races of domestic animals and plants and he began to wonder whether there might be some similar principle operating in nature. Various experiences in South America had left him, as we have seen, convinced that species could not be a series of immutable creations. How did one explain, then, the differences, small as they often were, between species?

Darwin hit accidentally on the answer late in 1838.

I happened to read for amusement Malthus on 'Population', and being well prepared to appreciate the struggle for existence which everywhere goes on from long-continued observation of the habits of animals and plants, it at once struck me that under these circumstances favourable variations would tend to be preserved, and unfavourable ones to be destroyed. The result of this would be the formation of a new species. Here, then, I had at last got a theory by which to work; but I was so anxious to avoid prejudice, that I determined not for some time to write even the briefest sketch of it.

In a moment of intuition, Darwin had discovered a new general principle; now began the labour of testing it with an ever increasing number of facts. It was only in June 1842 that he 'allowed himself the satisfaction' of putting his ideas on paper by 'writing a brief abstract of my theory in pencil in 35 pages; and this was enlarged during the summer of 1844 into one of 230 pages'. This 1844 essay is the fully written-out statement of his theory. Darwin still procrastinated, showing his essay to no one but Lyell and discussing his evolutionary ideas only with him and a few chosen friends, especially Hooker. He went on for many more years, building up an enormous collection of data on the subject. He interviewed people from all classes and professions and sent out questionnaires – all with a view to writing a book which would give the facts and arguments for and against his 'species theory'.

Darwin conducted his own experiments with the same end in mind. He compared the feet of tame and wild ducks; he built a pigeon house and stocked it with various breeds of pigeons. His object was, in his own words,

to view all facts that I can master (eheu, eheu, how ignorant I find I am

149

in Natural History) and on geographical distribution, palaeontology, classification, hybridism, domestic animals and plants, etc., etc. and to see how far they favour or are opposed to the notion that wild species are mutable or immutable; I mean with my utmost power to give all arguments and facts on both sides.

It is interesting to note how fair-minded he was, or professed to be, about the arguments for and against mutability. In 1856, urged by Lyell, Darwin began at long last to write his book; he always referred to it as his 'Big Book'. The title was to be *Natural Selection*. It is clear that he was a convinced evolutionist when in the company of fellow scientists. He wrote in that year to Asa Gray, the deeply religious professor of Botany at Harvard: 'As an honest man I must tell you that I have come to the heterodox conclusion that there are no such things as independently created species – that species are only strongly defined varieties. I know that this will make you despise me.'

Darwin had written nearly half the projected book when, on 18 June 1855, something happened that shook him profoundly. The postman brought a letter from Ternate in the Celebes Islands written by Alfred Russel Wallace, a brilliant young traveller naturalist, fourteen years younger than Darwin. With the letter there was a manuscript of an essay carrying the title, *On the tendency of variations to depart indefinitely from the Original Type.* This short essay was a perfect statement of Darwin's own theory of evolution by natural selection.

Alfred Russel Wallace has not, perhaps, been given as much credit as is his due for his independent discovery of the principle of natural selection. He was a good-natured, modest man and combined remarkable shrewdness in matters relating to natural history with credulity in dealing with human beings. As he advanced in age, he took up one cranky and unorthodox idea after the other; he became a phrenologist, anti-vaccinationist, spiritualist and socialist, with extreme ideas on the nationalization of land. These eccentricities did not show themselves when he was handling the facts of nature and speculating about the principles of evolutionary biology.

As a boy, Wallace dabbled in hypnotism, astronomy and botany. Two important events in his life were meeting Henry Walter Bates, the naturalist, and reading Malthus's *On Population* which for him, as for Darwin, was one of the foundations for the theory of natural selection. In 1848 he went with Bates on a collecting trip to the Amazon, where he was much impressed by

150

the majesty of the equatorial forests, the beauty of the butterflies and birds, and the contact with savage man. Later, in 1854, he went to the Malay Archipelago and stayed there eight years. It was there that he wrote, in 1855, his first contribution to the species problem – a paper entitled *Essay on the Law which has regulated the Introduction of New Species*. His main conclusion was that 'every species has come into existence coincident both in time and space with a pre-existing closely-allied species'. This essay was the most important 'pre-Darwinian' publication about the origin of species, apart from the works of Lamarck. It also showed that Wallace had, in fact, as complete a skeleton for a work on the origin of species as had Darwin when he wrote his first sketch in 1842. It was as a result of this essay that he started corresponding with Darwin,

The English carrier pigeon, also illustrated in Darwin's work on animals and plants under domestication.

Asa Gray, the professor of botany at Harvard University with whom Darwin corresponded.

who told him that he had, for a long time, been collecting facts with a bearing on the question of the origin of species, but without giving any hint of his theory of natural selection.

Although Wallace had been, for some time, a convinced evolutionist, it was only in 1858, when he was lying sick of malarial fever at Ternate, that the idea of natural selection as the solution of the *method* of evolution flashed upon him. He thought the whole thing out in a few hours, spent two days writing it down and then posted it to Darwin. Little did Wallace realize what a shattering effect his communication would have upon Darwin. In his letter he expressed the hope that 'the idea would be as new' to Darwin as

Henry Walter Bates was a friend of Darwin and in 1848 had explored Brazil with Wallace.

as it was to himself and asking him to forward the essay to Lyell if he thought it good enough. The paper arrived at a very bad time for Darwin: his youngest child had died of scarlet fever the day before and his little daughter Henrietta was dangerously ill with diphtheria. He wrote to Hooker, 'I am quite prostrated and can do nothing.'

Darwin forwarded Wallace's paper to Lyell the same day with the recommendation that it was 'well worth reading'. He went on,

Your words have come true with a vengeance – that I should be fore-stalled. You said this, when I explained to you here very briefly my views of 'Natural Selection' depending on the struggle for existence. I never

153

saw a more striking coincidence; if Wallace had my MS sketch written out in 1842, he could not have made a better short abstract! Even his terms now stand as heads of my chapters ... so all my originality, whatever it may amount to, will be smashed, though my book, if it will ever have any value, will not be deteriorated; as all the labour consists in the application of the theory.

A few days later he again wrote Lyell:

As I had not intended to publish my sketch, can I do so honourably, because Wallace has sent me an outline of his doctrine? I would far rather burn my whole book than that he or any other man should think that I behaved in a paltry spirit. Do you not think that his having sent me this sketch ties my hands?

The happy solution, which was due to the firm intervention of Hooker and Lyell, is sometimes spoken of as one of the noblest and most attractive episodes in the history of science. On 1 July 1858 the two papers, Darwin's and Wallace's, were read jointly to the Linnean Society of London and later published in the Society's Journal, under the title, '*On the Tendency of Species to form Varieties; and on the Perpetuation of Varieties and Species by Natural Means of Selection. By Charles Darwin,* Esq., FRS, FLS, and FGS, and *Alfred Wallace,* Esq., communicated by *Sir Charles Lyell,* FRS, FLS, and *J.D.Hooker,* Esq., MD, VPRS FLS, etc.' Had Hooker and Lyell not taken the matter into their hands, Darwin would certainly have refused to publish his views and we would not today be talking of Darwinism, but of Wallacism. Wallace always regarded Darwin as the originator of the theory of natural selection and he later, in 1889, published a popular exposition of the theory with the title, *Darwinism.* It was Wallace who called Darwin 'the Newton of Natural History'.

The joint paper made little impact on the scientific world.

Our joint production [wrote Darwin] excited very little attention, and the only published notice of them which I can remember was by Professor Haughton of Dublin, whose verdict was that all that was new in them was false, and what was true was old. This shows how necessary it is that any new view should be explained at considerable length in order to arouse public attention.

OPPOSITE Alfred Russel Wallace. He and Darwin formulated evolutionist theories independently but in a noble gesture presented their conclusions in a joint paper.

The President of the Linnean Society was also unaware that this joint paper was the opening salvo in the great evolutionary battle. At the annual general meeting he reported to members that, 'The year [1858] has not, indeed, been marked by any of those striking discoveries which at once revolutionise, so to speak, the department of science on which they bear.'

An illustration of the gibbon
from Huxley's account of
evolution.

156

The first result, then, of Wallace's unexpected and unwelcome letter was the joint announcement of their views to the Linnean Society. This, as we have seen, fell completely flat. The second result was the publication by Darwin of his *Origin of Species* in November of the following year, 1859.

The Origin of Species is the only one of Darwin's many books which the public has heard of. The catch-words 'natural selection', 'survival of the fittest', 'struggle for life', 'missing link', enter, at an early age, into the vocabularies of children. Some say that the effects of *The Origin* have been entirely bad, that Darwin pulled off a wicked and brilliant confidence trick by investing words like 'progress' and 'evolution' with a specious authority. It is only, they say, when these false notions can be shown to be the lies which they are, that human beings can perhaps be stopped in their reckless, moronic rush to the abyss and once again live their lives as they were lived in the old days – in mobile, self-sufficient communities, in tune with the precepts of the 'true philosophy' rather than with those of our present barbaric, bastard, pseudo-philosophy.

If Darwin's book has really had such malevolently destructive results and led to the warping of the human spirit, it deserves to be studied, just as *Mein Kampf* deserves to be studied – though we would presumably say that Hitler, the man of action, was more important than his book and that *The Origin of Species* was more important than its ailing author. It is interesting to look initially at one or two assertions in Darwin's autobiography, the text of which is as sacred for evolutionists as is the Old Testament for fundamentalists.

Darwin's conversion to the theory that species were not immutable, but had undergone gradual changes, dates from his first note-book written between July 1837 and February 1838. 'In July opened first note-book on Transmutation of Species. Had been greatly struck from about the previous March on character of South American fossils, and species on Galapagos Archipelago. These facts (especially latter), origin of all my views.' In these note-books he asked himself many questions – why animals and plants vary within the same species; why some species are born and others die; why species are related to each other and what is the link in their relationship. His tentative, groping answers to these questions were provided by his new theory of mutability.

Already, in the early days of the notebooks, Darwin was becoming emotionally committed to evolution, and conjecturing,

157

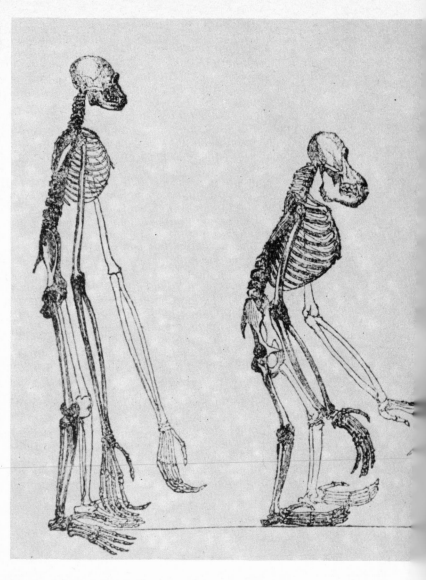

at first whimsically and then defiantly, about man's relationship
to the animals. 'If all men were dead, then monkeys make men, men
make angels.' This cryptic remark gives a novel twist to the later
controversy. Men are not the descendants, but the progenitors of
apes!

Let man visit orang-ou-tang in domestication, hear its expressive
whine, see its intelligence when spoken, as if it understood every word,
see its affection to those it knows, see its passion and rage, sulkiness and
despair; let him look at savage, roasting its parent, naked, artless, not

158

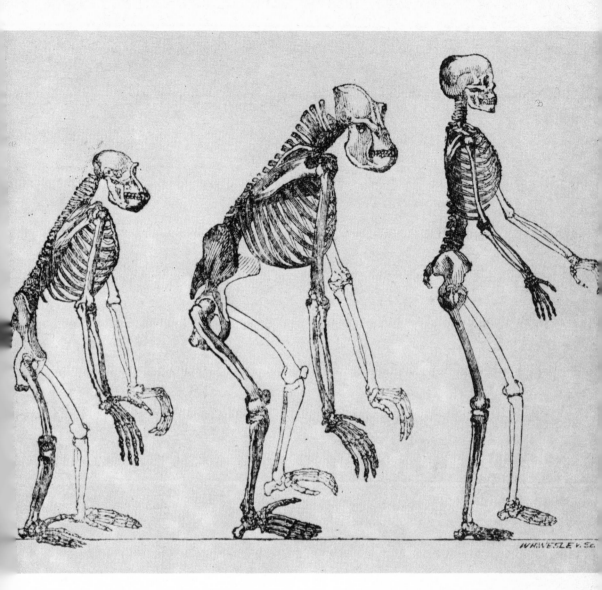

improving yet improvable; and then let him dare to boast of his proud preeminence. Man in his arrogance thinks himself a great work, worthy the interposition of a deity. More humble and I believe true to consider him created from animals.

There is something sinister and unpleasant in this naïve disparagement of human nature, as if the misanthrope is lurking somewhere in Darwin's bland and happy personality. Its tone is very different from his autobiographical account, touched on at the beginning of this chapter, describing the opening of his notebooks: 'My first note-book was opened in July 1837. I worked on true Baconian principles, and without any theory collected facts on a wholesale scale, more especially with respect to domesticated productions, by pointed enquiries, by conversation with skilful breeders and gardeners, and by extensive reading.'

The tools and methods which Darwin employed in his patient and indefatigable search for facts to prove or disprove his new theory would not have impressed the laboratory technician of today. They were, in fact, amateur by nineteenth-century standards and more suited to comfortably-off country gentlemen who dabbled in natural history. The children romped in his study as he examined the fibres of a plant with a simple microscope. The casualness of Darwin's fact-collecting methods is very endearing. He welcomed information from any source, provided it fitted into his new theory of mutability. His informants could be his father, his gardener, his pen-friends or anyone who had something helpful to say. 'Strong odour of negroes – a point of real repugnance.' 'The cat had its tail cut off at Shrewsbury and its kittens had all short tails; but one a little longer than the rest; they all died. She had kittens before and afterwards with tails.' The facts of which Darwin was so proud do not appear to have been collected or tested with any particular care. The vital factor was that they should illustrate his theory. In this respect Darwin was contradictory; at times he spoke as the dispassionate scientist, concerned only with the truth and prepared to jettison his beloved theory should the facts disprove it; at other times the theory was for him all-important and any facts would do, provided they supported it. In a letter to Lyell, shortly after the publication of *The Origin of Species*, he prided himself on having invented a theory and then seeing 'how many classes of facts the theory would explain'.

Darwin's originality and his contribution to scientific thought lay in his fearlessness in taking great intellectual leaps in the dark. He saw no point in looking for facts unless they could be welcomed in the embrace of some suggestive theory. 'How odd it is', he said, 'that anyone should not see that all observation must be for or against some view if it is to be of any service.' His influence on the thought of Victorians was due more to his ignorance of many fundamental matters than to his knowledge of them. He asked simple, basic, naïve questions about life. They were questions which experts would not presume to ask, let alone to answer. Darwin did both. He was free of the encumbrances of a detailed systematic knowledge of any branch of natural history, knowing far less than many of his fellow naturalists about species and varieties, comparative anatomy and other disciplines. With a simple, childlike directness, he asked questions about the origins of life. Such fundamental questions are usually asked by philosophers. Darwin himself admitted that metaphysical matters were too deep for his intelligence. The abstract thought of Coleridge or Kant was of no interest to him. He provided ready-made, down-to-earth answers to his basic questions and did not take any particular trouble to grasp the essence of the thought of the writers who influenced him.

At the beginning of this chapter, we found Darwin reading Malthus 'for amusement'. All of a sudden he stumbled on something which he had been looking for – natural selection. Was this an example of brilliant scientific intuition or of a facile aptitude for taking other people's ideas and deliberately or unwittingly distorting them? If the latter, it is unpleasantly reminiscent of the techniques of 'ideas men', one of the many curses of our present age. Malthus's book was called *An Essay on the Principle of Population*. At first sight, it appears unusual that Darwin should be indebted for his key theory to a book dealing with politics and economics. As a matter of fact, Malthus was as interested in natural history as he was in economics, and many passages of his book might well have been written by a naturalist. He discussed the theory that plants and animals were so prolific by nature that any one species would soon cover the whole earth if not held in check by other species:

Through the animal and vegetable kingdoms Nature has scattered the seeds of life abroad with the most profuse and liberal hand; but has been comparatively sparing in the room and the nourishment necessary to rear them. The germs of existence contained in this earth, if they could freely develop themselves, would fill millions of worlds in the course of a few thousand years. Necessity, that imperious, all-pervading law of nature, restrains them within the prescribed bounds. The race of plants and the race of animals shrink under this great restrictive law; and man cannot by any effort of reason escape from it.

Malthus described how civilized peoples were often compelled to leave overcrowded communities and make for less-populated areas, whose inhabitants would, in their turn, feel threatened by their arrival and that many 'struggles for existence' would then ensue. Darwin took over the expression 'struggle for existence' or 'struggle for life' and equated it with the 'survival of the fittest'. This could be regarded as a distortion of Malthus, who never

161

Vegetation of Islas Plazas in the Galapagos Islands: red lichen, grey matforming lichen and the Opuntia Echio cactus.

Marine iguanas seen by Darwin in the Galapagos Islands.

suggested that races would improve in strength and quality in consequence of these struggles. On the contrary, he wished to show that human society would never move far towards perfection, because its tendency to multiply beyond its means of subsistence would keep it in a permanent state of misery and degradation. He did not believe in the idea of progress, whether applied to plants, animals or human beings.

Darwin took several of Malthus's ideas and used them quite differently. For example, instead of, like Malthus, giving the struggle for existence as an explanation of the tragic character of the human situation, he did the exact opposite. According to Darwin, the struggle for existence, or the principle of natural selection, was the means whereby species were constantly changing and improving; the strong, or the fittest, survived and the weak died out.

It was, it will be remembered, in 1842 that Darwin 'allowed himself the satisfaction' of writing a brief sketch of his theory, which was enlarged in 1844. Then followed those fifteen long years during which he painstakingly accumulated evidence in support of his theory. We have already heard much about his pathological reluctance to present his findings to the world until they had been submitted to every kind of test. Those out to 'debunk' Darwin might say that his book, when it finally appeared, was not much fuller than the enlarged sketch of 1844. Even the rough sketch of 1842 covered most of the ground of *The Origin* and it even wound up with the following purple passage, which was very like the memorable final paragraph of the great book and also recalled Erasmus's vision of evolution in *Zoonomia*.

It accords with what we know of the law impressed on matter by the Creator, that the creation and extinction of forms, like the birth and death of individuals, should be the effect of secondary means. It is derogatory that the Creator of countless systems of worlds should have created each of the myriads of creeping parasites and slimy worms which have swarmed each day of life on land and water on this one globe. We cease being astonished, however much we may deplore, that a group of animals should have been directly created to lay their eggs in bowels and flesh of others, – that some organisms should delight in cruelty, – that animals should be led away by false instincts, – that annually there should be an incalculable waste of eggs and pollen. From death, famine, rapine, and the concealed war of nature, we can see that the highest good, which we can conceive, the creation of the higher animals has directly come. Doubtless it at first transcends our humble powers, to conceive laws capable of creating individual organisms, each characterised by the most exquisite

OPPOSITE Part of the manu-script of the *Origin of Species*.

Autograph of Charles Darwin

I have now recapitulated the chief facts and considerations, which have thoroughly convinced me that species have been modified, during a long course of descent, by the preservation or the natural selection of many successive slight favourable variations. I cannot believe that a false theory could explain, as it seems to me that the the theory of natural selection does explain, the several large classes of facts above specified. It is a valid objection that science as yet throws no light on the far higher problem of the essence or origin of life. Who can explain what is the essence of attraction of gravity? No one now objects to following out the results consequent on this unknown element of attraction; notwithstanding that Leibnitz formerly accused Newton of introducing "occult qualities & miracles into philosophy." —

Charles Darwin

p 514 3ᵈ Edit.
of "Origin"

workmanship and widely-extended adaptations. It accords better with the lowness of our faculties to suppose that each must require the fiat of a creator, but in the same proportion the existence of such laws should exalt our notion of the power of the omniscient Creator. There is a simple grandeur in the view of life with its powers of growth, assimilation and reproduction, being originally breathed into matter under one or a few forms, and that whilst this our planet has gone circling on according to fixed laws, and land and water, in a cycle of change, have gone on replacing each other, that form so simple an origin, through the process of gradual selection of infinitesimal changes, endless forms most beautiful and most wonderful have been evolved.

What was Darwin doing all this time if he was not, as the legend goes, building pile upon pile of incontrovertible facts in support of his theory? He was taking things more easily than his impatient biographers and perhaps even, from time to time, putting his species work out of his mind. After he had finished work on his *Journals* and on *The Geology of South America*, he turned his attention to cirrepedia, or barnacles. He wanted to clear up one or two points about a certain barnacle found on the coast of Chile and he expected the work to take him a couple of months. This led to the study of the whole group of barnacles which lasted eight years and led to the publication of the standard reference works on the subject. He became steadily more immersed in them and had at one moment ten thousand barnacles which had been sent to him from various countries. His children could not visualize a life without barnacles. When one of his sons visited some neighbours near Downe, he asked the little boy where his father did his barnacles.

The eight years from 1846 to 1854 which Darwin spent on barnacles turned him, so he claimed, into a 'complete naturalist'. Huxley and others praised his courage and application in submitting himself, relatively late in life, to such detailed training in the biology and anatomy of these tiny creatures. Although the barnacle years cannot be dignified as a carefully-prepared plan to make good Darwin's deficiences in different scientific fields, they happened to have this effect. He realised, for the first time, how difficult it was to distinguish species from varieties: 'After describing a set of forms as distinct species, tearing up my Ms and making them one species, tearing that up and making them separate, and then making them one again (which has happened to me), I have gnashed my teeth, cursed species, and asked what sin I had committed to be so punished.'

166

Darwin also spent the years between his second draft and the publication of *The Origin* in carrying on an enormous correspondence with every kind of person – relations, strangers, scientists, cranks. In this way he amassed a great deal of heterogeneous information, much of which he would not otherwise have collected. Apart from breeding pigeons, Darwin did not feel up to conducting experiments himself and he relied a great deal on these gleanings from correspondents. In his letters, Darwin asked every sort of question. 'At what age do nestling pigeons have their tail feathers sufficiently developed to be counted?' 'Did you ever see black greyhound (or any sub-breed) with tan feet, and a tan coloured spot over inner corner of each eye? I want such cases, and such *must* exist because theory tells me it ought.' He was grateful for any presents, such as the carcase of a half-bred African cat.

The three friends and fellow-scientists whose support Darwin desperately needed for his theory were Hooker, Lyell and Huxley. Of these, Lyell was for Darwin the least satisfactory. He shifted his ground too often. At times he appeared to be converted to mutability; at other times he suspended judgment, not so much because he had doubts about the theory but because he dreaded the social consequences. Once the masses were told that they need no longer believe that species were separate and independent creations, there was no knowing into what dangerous ways their new-found intellectual liberty might lead them.

Hooker caused Darwin less anxiety than did Lyell. He was a great systematic botanist, and Darwin depended very much on his knowledge of plants. When Hooker visited Downe, it was, he wrote,

an established rule that he every day pumped me, as he called it, for half an hour or so after breakfast in his study, when he first brought out a heap of slips with questions botanical, geographical etc. for me to answer, and concluded by telling me of the progress he had made in his own work, asking my opinion on various prints.

Darwin said of Hooker's visits: 'I learn more in these discussions than in ten times over the number of hours reading.' Hooker came at times very close to being a co-author of *The Origin of Species*. He read and criticized it chapter by chapter and supplied Darwin with all the facts he needed on subjects like the variation, transportation and cross-fertilization of plants. Darwin's son later said that 'without Hooker's aid Darwin's great work would hardly have been carried out on the botanical side'. Hooker, however, was

OVERLEAF Darwin together with Lyell (centre) and Hooker (right) who encouraged him to publish his views on evolution.

not prepared to go the whole way with Darwin as far as mutability was concerned. He accepted that there was considerable variability in species and also their relationship to fossil predecessors, but he still preferred to accept the old fundamental theory of the fixity of species.

Of the three confidants, Huxley was the one most likely to espouse Darwin's theory, being self-made, iconoclastic and adventurous by temperament. Yet he held out for a long time, believing in evolution within, but not between, species. He came to accept Darwin's theory fully only after reading both the joint Darwin/Wallace paper to the Linnean Society and *The Origin* itself.

MONKEYANA.

AM. I
A
MAN AND
A
BROTHER?

Am I satyr or man?
Pray tell me who can,
And settle my place in the scale.
A man in ape's shape,
An anthropoid ape,
Or monkey deprived of his tail?

7
The Storm Breaks

The *Vestiges* taught,
That all came from naught
By "development," so called, "progressive;"
That insects and worms
Assume higher forms
By modification excessive.

Then DARWIN set forth.
In a book of much worth,
The importance of "Nature's selection;"
How the struggle for life
Is a laudable strife,
And results in "specific distinction."

Let pigeons and doves
Select their own loves,
And grant them a million of ages,
Then doubtless you'll find
They've altered their kind,
And changed into prophets and sages.

LEONARD HORNER relates,
That Biblical dates
The age of the world cannot trace;
That Bible tradition,
By Nile's deposition,
Is put to the right about face.

Then there's PENGELLY
Who next will tell ye
That he and his colleagues of late
Find celts and shaped stones
Mixed up with cave bones
Of contemporaneous date.

Then PRESTWICH, he pelts
With hammers and celts
All who do not believe his relation,
That the tools he exhumes
From gravelly tombs
Date before the Mosaic creation.

Then HUXLEY and OWEN,
With rivalry glowing,
With pen and ink rush to the scratch;
'Tis Brain *versus* Brain,
Till one of them's slain;
By Jove! it will be a good match!

Says OWEN, you can see
The brain of Chimpanzee
Is always exceedingly small,
With the hindermost "horn"
Of extremity shorn,
And no "Hippocampus" at all.

The Professor then tells 'em,
That man's "cerebellum,"
From a vertical point you can't see;
That each "convolution"
Contains a solution,
Of "Archencephalic" degree

Then apes have no nose,
And thumbs for great toes,
And a pelvis both narrow and slight;
They can't stand upright,
Unless to show fight,
With "DU CHAILLU," that chivalrous knight!

Next HUXLEY replies,
That OWEN he lies,
And garbles his Latin quotation;
That his facts are not new,
His mistakes not a few,
Detrimental to his reputation.

" To twice slay the slain,"
By dint of the Brain,
(Thus HUXLEY concludes his review)
Is but labour in vain,
Unproductive of gain,
And so I shall bid you "Adieu!"

Zoological Gardens, May, 1861.   GORILLA.

The *Origin of Species* was completed by the spring of 1859. 'We have set up a billiards table, and I find it does me a deal of good, and drives the horrid species out of my head.'

Darwin considered his book to be merely an 'Abstract' of the 'Big Book' and he was very disappointed at his publisher, John Murray, objecting to use of the word 'Abstract' in the title. He took great trouble about the 'promotion' of his book, arranging for advance copies to be sent to eminent foreign naturalists when he was recovering from the exhaustion of proof-reading at a water-cure establishment at Ilkley.

The *Origin of Species* was published on 24 November 1859 and the whole edition of 1,250 copies was sold out the same day. So nervous had Darwin been about its reception, that he told John Murray that he would free him from any obligation to publish if he thought it might lead to a financial loss. As it was, such was the demand that a second edition of three thousand copies was published two months later and a sixth and final edition came out in 1882.

Darwin, unwittingly, chose the right moment for the publication of his book. The doctrine of the immutability of species appeared, to thoughtful members of the upper-middle classes, to be steadily less probable as the implications of the findings of the great geologists became clearer. They expected someone to take a lead in relating to each other the discoveries of the geologists and the biologists. Strangely enough, Darwin never once mentioned 'evolution' in his book. The word first appeared in his *The Descent of Man*, written two years later. When asked by Wallace whether he proposed to discuss 'man' in *The Origin of Species*, he said that he intended to avoid the subject as it was too much surrounded by prejudices. He contented himself by remarking at the very end of the book, 'Much light will be thrown on the origin of man and his history.' He was most anxious, if it could be avoided, not to offend the religious feelings of his wife, his friends and the general public. His sensitive nature recoiled from any kind of controversy.

Many learned and educated people saw, however, that the issue *did* concern man and they feared that Darwin's book, by ignoring the moral and metaphysical idea of life, might lead us into a state of degradation and materialism. It could destroy our faith in the Bible and turn us into brutes. Time has shown that there is something in this. We live now in a world of agnostic materialism and the unfortunate Darwin has been appropriated by the Russians, as was Wagner by the Nazis. Both men would have

PREVIOUS PAGES A contemporary cartoon and verse from *Punch* parodying the well-known anti-slavery cameo issued by Wedgwood which showed a negro slave with the inscription, 'Am I not a man and a brother?'

been surprised at being adopted as mascots of such crude ideologies.

We hear so much about the 'furore' caused in Victorian England by Darwin's book. Was this indignation expressed at all levels of society or confined to chatter at high-tables? Although Darwin's contemporaries were ready for an evolution theory, they were not ready for the one with which he presented them. They were not prepared to accept the theory of natural selection, which could do without a supernatural element to explain away inconsistencies. Like the Frenchman Laplace, his answer to anyone who asked how God fitted into his scheme would have been, 'Sire, je n'ai pas besoin de cette hypothèse' ('Sir, I do not need this hypothesis'). Darwin had also to contend with the feelings and prejudices of distinguished scientists – even of his friend Lyell – who insisted that supernatural explanations were as valid as scientific ones.

The book, as its sales figures have demonstrated, caused an immediate stir among the middle classes. The masses could not have been expected to read a book costing £1 and crammed with facts and sustained reasoning. *The Origin of Species* was ignored in the popular press and reviewed in only the more expensive newspapers.

The interest of the public in Darwin's theory was, needless to say, shallow and prejudiced. Few people really cared one way or the other whether animal and plant species were transmutable or not. When, however, the question became bound up with the possibility of man's descent from the lower animals; when it appeared to be challenging the Bible's explanation of the origin of living things – then the popular press saw that it was on to a good thing and alarmed and titillated its readers with Darwin's 'Ape Theory'. The national 'debate' was on whether man was descended from Adam or from the apes. Although, therefore, interest in the scientific originality of *The Origin of Species* was limited to those qualified to understand such matters, the book achieved a large sale because it became associated with questions relating to religion and to the interpretation of Nature. The popular press was soon full of articles about gorillas and the 'missing link' between men and apes. It was in 1864 that Disraeli, with his instinctive politician's grasp of the mentality of the middle-classes, stated in a speech at Oxford that the question was whether man was an ape or an angel. As we all know, he answered his question with the words, 'I am on the side of the angels.'

The controversy first came into the open at a meeting of the

Birds Pl 34

Tanagra Darwini

LEFT Tanagra Darwinii, found feeding on the fruit of an opuntia at Maldonado *(top)*; Chlorospiza Melano-dera, found in the East Falkland Islands and at Santa Cruz, Patagonia *(bottom)*.

OPPOSITE Rhea Darwinii: Darwin first noticed the bird in Rio Negro when he heard the Gauchos talking about a rare bird. This one was accidentally shot and eaten by Martens who did not appreciate its rarity. It was reconstructed from the remains!

Birds Pl 32

Rhea Darwinii.

A cartoon inspired by the debate on
Darwinism, entitled 'The Darwinian Theory –
a Sketch in the Monkey-House of the
Zoological Gardens'.

British Association in Oxford in June 1860. As was only to be expected, Darwin felt too ill to come to the meeting. *The Origin of Species* had been out six months and was becoming increasingly the subject of hushed and scandalized conversations. 'Soapy Sam' Wilberforce, the Bishop of Oxford, addressing the meeting, spoke in complacent and supercilious tones about Darwin's theories. Carried away by the apparent success of his wit and eloquence, he turned to Huxley and asked him whether it was 'through his grandfather or his grandmother that he claimed descent from a monkey?' Huxley, who enjoyed this sort of situation, rose and stated gravely that Darwin's theories about species were about the most convincing that anyone had as yet put forward. He then answered the Bishop's taunt: 'If the question is put to me, would I rather have a miserable ape for a grandfather or a man highly endowed by nature and possessing great means for the mere purpose of introducing ridicule into a grave scientific discussion – I unhesitatingly affirm my preference for the ape.' Huxley later commented that his retort caused 'inextinguishable laughter among the people, and they listened to the rest of my argument with great attention'.

Darwin's scrupulous avoidance of the vexed subject of man and his origins had availed him nothing. Prelates, scientists and editors had chosen to construe his book as an attack on the divine origin of man. The sterile and ignorant controversy continued throughout the 1860s. When he published his *Descent of Man* in 1871, it was nothing like the sensation that the *Origin* had been, twelve years earlier. The public was getting tired of the argument.

'As soon as I had become, in the year 1837 or 1838, convinced that species were mutable productions, I could not avoid the belief that man must come under the same law. Accordingly, I collected notes on the subject for my own satisfaction, and not for a long time with any intention of publishing'. The steady shift of interest towards the question of man's evolution was shown in various publications which followed *The Origin of Species*. In 1863, Huxley published *Evidence as to Man's Place in Nature* which established, by anatomical comparisons, the relationship between man and the anthropoid apes. The following year, Wallace published a paper in which he affirmed that man was no exception to the laws of evolution and that natural selection had made him what he was. He hesitated to apply this to man's brain which had, he thought been developed by non-evolutionary means. Darwin told Wallace 'that the struggle between the races of man depended

OPPOSITE Bishop Wilberforce, whose high-flown attack on Darwinism met with a strong retort from Huxley.

entirely on intellectual and *moral* qualities'. He was a fervent
believer in the White Man's Burden. He opposed birth-control as
interfering with the workings of natural selection and also because
it would deprive large areas of the world of the benefits of British
rule: 'No words can exaggerate the importance, in my opinion, of
our colonization for the future history of the world.'

A large part of *The Descent of Man* was devoted to the abstruse
subject of sexual selection. Here again, Wallace gave another
example of his brilliance of insight. Darwin was trying to explain
the bright colouring of animals by his theory of sexual selection.
He came to the vivid hues of caterpillars, only to find that they had,
at this stage, no sex life at all! In his perplexity, he turned to
Wallace who, by return of post, sent his theory of warning
colorations, which is accepted today. Darwin told him, 'You are
the man to apply to in a difficulty.'

The year 1870, during which he prepared for publication *The
Descent of Man* was an exceptionally busy one in his life. In case we
forget his perennial grumbles, he wrote Hooker in June,

I am glad you were at the 'Messiah'; it is the one thing I should like to
hear again, but I daresay I should find my soul too dried up to appreciate
it as in the old days; and that I should feel very flat, for it is a horrid bore
to feel as I constantly do, that I am a withered leaf for every subject
except science. It sometimes makes me hate science, though God knows
I ought to be thankful for such a perennial interest, which makes me
forget for some hours every day my accursed stomach.

Darwin's main argument in the *Descent of Man* is that man is not
a created, but an evolved form. When the application of his doctrines to man, as opposed to the lower organisms, was debated, the
anti-Darwinians had no need to base their case on scientific
argument. They had two convenient lines of attack, both aimed at
feelings, fears and prejudices. One was the 'religious' approach,
which led to many entertaining blasts of theological fury. A newspaper recalled the conflict between the Catholic Church and
Galileo; while admitting that speculations could sometimes lead to
great discoveries, it was otherwise 'with speculations which
trench upon sacred ground, and which run counter to the univer-
sal convictions of mankind, poisoning the fountains of science,
and disturbing the serenity of the Christian world'. Another
commented, 'Society must fall to pieces if Darwinism be true.' The
Edinburgh Review and *The Times*, neither religious papers, issued
strong warnings about the religious and social consequences of
the *Descent of Man*:

180

It is impossible to over-estimate the magnitude of the issue. If our humanity be merely the natural product of the modified faculties of the brutes, most earnest-minded men will be compelled to give up those motives by which they have attempted to live noble and virtuous lives, as founded on a mistake ... our moral sense will turn out to be a mere developed instinct ... and the revelation of God to us, and the hope of a future life, pleasurable daydreams invented for the good of society. If these views be true, a revolution in thought is imminent, which will shake society to its very foundation by destroying the sanctity of the conscience and the religious sense.

A man incurs grave responsibility who, with the authority of a well-earned reputation, advances at such a time the disintegrating speculations of this book. He ought to be capable of supporting them by the most conclusive evidence of facts. To put them forward on much incomplete evidence, such cursory investigation, such hypothetical arguments as we have exposed, is more than unscientific – it is reckless.

The other anti-Darwinian approach was to excite feelings of revulsion at the thought of a genetic relationship existing between us and the brutes. To believe such a thing was, according to one newspaper, a 'mental catastrophe'. Those who spread such a belief were out 'to degrade man deeply in the scale of animal existence'. Wallace's suggestion that some other power, *not* Natural Selection, had formed man's mental and moral faculties, gave considerable pleasure to the anti-Darwinians. One newspaper lost no time in saying that, 'Mr Wallace's reference ... to a Creator's will really undermines Mr Darwin's whole hypothesis.' The Darwinian controversy thus moved away from the physical and more toward the mental and spiritual state of man. Darwin's opponents believed themselves to be on stronger ground when stating that Natural Selection could not be made to apply to man's mental powers. Such powers, they argued, were of no practical use to him in his savage state. 'No mere exigencies of life or struggle for existence can have given rise to the high thoughts which led to poetry and science. How would the conception of space and time, of form, beauty, and order, above all, of right and wrong, be of any use to a savage in his early struggle for existence?' 'The brain of savage man is far beyond his needs ... if it once originated, it ought, according to Mr Darwin's Theory, to have been lost by disuse!'

These critics did not generally distinguish between the human mind and the human soul. The main thing was that there were elements which kept man apart from the brutes. Various writers drew up lists of those faculties which were specifically human –

Another *Punch* cartoonist's
view of the controversy.

the power of telling good from evil, of generalizing, of language, of conceiving God, etc. Catholics had merely to refer to St Thomas Aquinas to find convincing anti-Darwinian material:

The souls of brutes being entirely dependent upon their bodies, it follows that they can have no ideas higher than those which can be acquired by means of the senses. Man, on the other hand, is endowed with the power of subjecting the ideas obtained from his senses to analysis and by abstraction, at arriving at the knowledge of the essence of the object represented to him from without. This is a perfectly distinct faculty from anything to be found in the brutes.

The Darwinian defence to these attacks was simply to take a

A Lecture, — "You will at once perceive, continued Professor Ichthyosaurus, that the
some of the lower order of animals the teeth are very insignificant the power of the jaws
seems wonderful how the creature could have procured food."

A cartoon that appeared twenty-eight
years before the publication of the
Origin. Evolution was already being
discussed but the prevailing attitude
was one of scepticism.

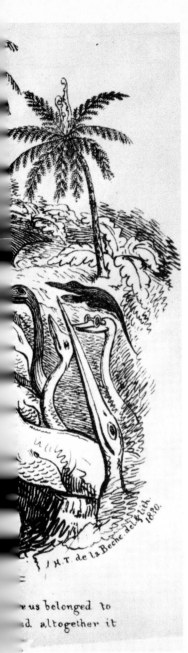

e us belonged to
d altogether it

stand on scientific methods of enquiry. When Darwin compared the faculties of men and animals, his standard of comparison was their outward behaviour. If their behaviour was similar, he assumed that their thoughts were similar. He hoped to show in this way that there was no important difference between animal instincts and human reason. He admitted that there was a considerable difference between animals and men in mental powers, but this was a difference of degree and not of kind. This could be best illustrated by studying, as he had in the case of his own child, the development of human infants. They slowly acquire the 'higher faculties'.

The shattering impact of Darwinism on mid-Victorian Protestantism is one of the most famous episodes in our intellectual history. The shock still lingers. It was only in 1968 that the State Legislature of Tennessee abolished its anti-evolution laws and it was no longer illegal to teach evolution in schools. We know that the last thing Darwin wanted was that his scientific views should cause distress to religious people. That he should have been surprised when they did may suggest that he was deficient in religious feeling.

Darwin had not given much thought to religious problems since those days at Cambridge when he was so impressed by Paley's *Evidences*. He seldom, if ever, discussed religious questions in his books. Towards the end of his life he allowed himself to be drawn on the subject:

What my own views may be is a question of no consequence to any one but myself. But, as you ask, I may state that my judgment often fluctuates. … In my most extreme fluctuations I have never been an Atheist in the sense of denying the existence of a God. I think that generally (and more and more as I grow older), but not always, that an Agnostic would be the most correct description of my state of mind.

He gave his bad health as a reason which prevented him from feeling 'equal to deep reflection, on the deepest subject which can fill a man's mind'. In 1873, he answered a Dutch student who wanted to have his views on religion:

I may say that the impossibility of conceiving that this grand and wondrous universe, with our conscious selves, arose through chance, seems to me the chief argument for the existence of God; but whether this is an argument of real value, I have never been able to decide. I am aware that if we admit a first cause, the mind still craves to know whence it came, and how it arose nor can I overlook the difficulty from this immense amount of suffering through the world. I am, also, induced to defer

185

to a certain extent to the judgment of the many able men who have fully believed in God; but here again I see how poor an argument this is. The safest conclusion seems to me that the whole subject is beyond the scope of man's intellect; but man can do his duty.

Later, a German student wrote asking for information about his religious beliefs. His letter was answered by a member of the family on Darwin's behalf, stating his view that evolution was compatible with belief in God, although different persons had different ideas of what they meant by God. The German youth, not satisfied with this explanation, wrote again to Darwin, who, this time, replied personally:

I am much engaged, an old man, and out of health, and I cannot spare time to answer your questions fully – nor indeed can they be answered. Science has nothing to do with Christ, except in so far as the habit of scientific research makes a man cautious in admitting evidence. For myself, I do not believe that there has ever been any revelation. As for a future life, every man must judge for himself between conflicting vague probabilities.

Darwin more or less gave up his belief in a personal God after he had discovered the law of natural selection: 'There seems to be no more design in the variability of organic beings, and in the action of natural selection, than in the course which the wind blows.' He told a story about his father, whom an old lady suspected of unorthodoxy. She hoped to convert him with the words, 'Doctor, I know that sugar is sweet in my mouth, and I know that my Redeemer liveth.'

Darwin was not in the least bit anxious to influence theological speculation; if the *Origin of Species* did so, this was an unintended side-effect. The threat which it offered to Victorian Anglicanism has also been exaggerated – this is not surprising with a public which depends for nourishment on crude half-truths and simple melodrama. Tennyson, in *In Memoriam*, written in 1850, had spoken of 'Nature, red in tooth and claw':

> Are God and Nature then at strife,
> That Nature lends such evil dreams?
> So careful of the type she seems,
> So careless of the single life ...

Tennyson thought a lot about evolution and the struggle for life, but it is not certain how much this affected his religious doubts and difficulties. The spectacle of Nature's brutality and destruc-

Darwin himself became the target for much ridicule. This cartoon is from the *London Sketch Book*.

187

tiveness already seemed to many Victorians to be incompatible with the existence of a personal God.

Edmund Gosse, in *Father and Son*, described how the evolutionary crisis racked his father's spirit. Philip Gosse was a distinguished marine biologist and a fanatical fundamentalist. In 1857, there was taking place a quiet recruitment of forces. It would soon be necessary to stand in one army or the other. In that year the question was first asked, 'What, then, did we come from, an orang-outang?' Hooker and Lyell wished to initiate a few naturalists, who were expert in the description of species, in the new doctrines of natural selection which Darwin was shortly to give to the world. Philip Gosse's first instinct was to greet with enthusiasm this subtle and convincing new doctrine. He then remembered the opening chapter of *Genesis* and resolved to have nothing more to do with this terrible new theory but to stick tenaciously to the law of the fixity of species. As his son said, 'By a strange act of wilfulness, he closed the doors upon himself for ever.'

Philip Gosse's answer to Lyell was *Omphalos*, a book which would explain geology to the godly readers of *Genesis*. Its argument was that there had been no gradual modification of the earth's surface, but a sudden, catastrophic act of creation, the world appearing as a planet in which life had long existed. To Gosse's pain, his book was greeted with ridicule by atheists and Christians alike. If he had chosen biology for his experiment in reaction, he might have met with greater success. In geology it was less dangerous to indulge in evolutionary speculations. In *Omphalos*, Adam had a navel, and the earth was complete with all the rock-layers and fossils which it would have contained had evolution actually occurred.

Philip Gosse's theological views were, however, those of a tiny minority and the mirth which they provoked showed that the Victorians were in a receptive mood for the advent of Darwinism. The last paragraph of *The Origin of Species,* so heavily pondered and close in its reasoning, is a far cry from the semi-deranged biblical fanaticism of *Omphalos*:

It is interesting to contemplate a tangled bank, clothed with many plants of many kinds, with birds singing on the bushes, with various insects flitting about, and with worms crawling through the damp earth, and to reflect that these elaborately constructed forms, so different from each other, and dependent upon each other in so complex a manner, have all been produced by laws acting around us. These laws, taken in the

OPPOSITE A cartoon of Darwin in the 1860s.

189

largest sense, being Growth with Reproduction; Inheritance which is almost implied by reproduction; Variability from the indirect and direct action of the conditions of life, and from use and disuse; a ratio of increase so high as to lead to a Struggle for Life, and as a consequence to Natural Selection, entailing Divergence of Character and the Extinction of less-improved forms. Thus, from the war of nature, from famine and death, the most exalted object which we are capable of conceiving, namely, the production of the higher animals, directly follows. There is grandeur in this view of life, ... that, whilst this planet has gone cycling on according to the fixed laws of gravity, from so simple a beginning, endless forms most beautiful and most wonderful have been, and are being evolved.

8 The Riddle of Darwin

SUDDENLY, AT THE LATEISH AGE OF FIFTY, the invalid naturalist was a celebrity. Byron was only twenty-four when he 'woke up one morning and found himself famous'. The success of Darwin's book depended on its 'authoritative' character, on convincing the public that many years of patient endeavour had been spent in the steady accumulation of innumerable facts. To this extent, it was necessary that he should already have gained a reputation among scientists.

The patient, humble and ailing seer, in his black coat and black wide-brimmed hat, unable to take more than a few steps without support – this was the 'image' which Darwin presented to the Victorian public for the last twenty years of his life and which persists today. Had we not known him better, we might almost think that he had been brilliantly successful in 'backing into the limelight'. After dethroning the God of Abraham, and Christ, Who sat on His right side, he allowed all those Victorian agnostics to invest him with those qualities for which their bereaved souls were yearning. Overnight, he acquired both the look of Moses or, if you prefer, Wotan, and the humble attributes of the Lamb. Christ-like, he meekly bore the howls of execration which greeted his book, and God-like, he silenced his critics by his awesome serenity. On seeing his portrait in 1875, he wrote to Hooker: 'I look a very venerable, acute, melancholy old dog; whether I really look so I do not know.'

Be that as it may, Darwin, whatever his 'image' then or now, continued until his death to work and to write on all types of organic phenomena: botany, for example. The scope and influence of Darwin's botanical work have been overshadowed by his biological and geological discoveries. He began to study plants because he found that he could observe in them certain organic processes in their least complicated forms. He approached the subject in the spirit of an amateur. This, in the words of William Thistleton Dyer, Hooker's son-in-law and successor at Kew, was of great importance for,

from not being till he took up any point, familiar with the literatures bearing on it, his mind was absolutely free from any prepossession. He was never afraid of his facts, or of framing any hypothesis, however startling, which seemed to explain them ... his long experience had given him a kind of instinctive insight into the method of attack of any biological problem, however unfamiliar to him, while he rigidly controlled the fertility of his mind in hypothetical explanations by the no less fertility of ingeniously devised experiment.

Darwin loved plants as passionately as he did worms and beetles. As early as 1839, when he was collecting facts for his species theory, he was attracted to the cross-fertilization of flowers by insects. He saw a connection between the study of flowers and the problem of evolution: 'I was led to attend to the cross-fertilization of flowers by the aid of insects, from having come to the conclusion in my speculations on the origin of species, that crossing played an important part in keeping specific forms constant.' In 1862 Darwin published *On the various contrivances by which British and foreign orchids are fertilized by insects*, this being, incidentally, the only one of his books published in plum instead of the usual dark green cloth. This was followed in the same year by a paper for the journal of the Linnean Society, *Two forms, on dimorphic condition, in the species of primula*. He enjoyed the ten months which he spent writing this delightful little book. 'They are wonderful creatures, these Orchids, and I sometimes think with a glow of pleasure, when I remember making out some little point in their methods of fertilization.' Darwin's book on orchids was praised in all quarters, the only faint criticism coming from a religious newspaper, which said that his expressions of admiration for the contrivances of orchids were too indirect a way of saying 'O Lord, how manifold are Thy works.'

In 1865 he wrote *On the movement and habits of climbing plants*. His new hobby was to observe the activities of the tendrils of plants. 'It is strange, but I really think no one has explained simple twining plants ... the only approach to work which I can do is to look at tendrils and climbers, this does not distress my weakened brain.' *The variation in animals and plants under domestication* was published in 1868. Darwin had begun to write it in 1860. Its object was to show what kinds of changes had been brought about under artificial conditions of selection since the domestication of animals and the cultivation of plants had been practised. He did not treat plants in such detail as animals in this book, although he did point out and explain why no useful plants had come from Australia, New Zealand, North America and other places. It was in this book that he advanced the hypothesis of Pangenesis, 'which implies that the whole organization, in the sense of every separate atom or unit, reproduces itself. Hence ovules and pollen – grains – the fertilized seed or egg, as well as buds – include and consist of a multitude of germs thrown off from each separate atom of the organism.'

Darwin's hypothesis of Pangenesis (an identical theory had

been put forward in Greece about 400 BC) is today discredited. It has been suggested that he would have avoided several pitfalls had he paid attention to Mendel's paper on the genetics of the pea which he read to the Natural History Society of Brünn in 1865. Mendel possessed the third German edition of *The Origin of Species*, published in 1863, and he marked in it those passages which dealt with variation and the origins of hybrids.

Insectivorous Plants, published in 1875, goes back to one summer day in 1860 when Darwin noticed how many insects were caught by the common sun-dew plant (Drosera rotundifolia): 'I carried home some plants and on giving them insects, saw the movements of the tentacles, and this made me think it probable that the insects were caught for some special purpose.' Most species of Drosera grow in boggy places; for cultivation, they are best treated as greenhouse plants. Although often rather beautiful, they are really interesting on account of their carnivorous habits. The insect is entrapped by the sensitive hairs of the leaf which curl round it and the leaf spreads open again after digestion is complete. Darwin was fascinated by this plant: 'I care more about Drosera than the origin of all the species in the world.' An extraordinary fact about Drosera was that after the fly had been caught and the glands secreted digestive juice on to it, the products of the digested insect were absorbed by the glands and passed into the tissues of the plant. 'By Jove,' said Darwin, 'I sometimes think Drosera is a disguised animal!'

Although Darwin was not a professional botanist, he was happier, perhaps, when observing the habits of living plants than when doing anything else. He used to stand in front of a plant and gaze at it affectionately. His gardener had no use for such behaviour. When asked about his master's health, he replied 'Oh! my poor master has been very sadly. I often wish he had something to do. He moons about in the garden, and I have seen him standing doing nothing before a flower for ten minutes at a time. If he only had something to do I really believe he would be better.'

In 1875 Darwin published *The effects of cross- and self-fertilization in the vegetable kingdom*. He had laboured doggedly in his efforts to discover the significance of cross-fertilization. At last he had done so; in experiments conducted over twelve years on fifty-seven species of plants, he found that the products of cross-pollination were more numerous, fertile and vigorous than those of self-pollination. It later transpired that the very same experiments which he had carried out in the garden at Down

Otus Galapagoensis, found on James Island, Galapagos. This owl differed from European ones in its smaller size and darker colouring.

House had been made in the same year by Mendel in the garden of his monastery at Brünn in Czechoslovakia.

Finally, he published, in 1880, with the help of his son Francis, *The power of movement in plants*. This he described as

a tough piece of work ... in accordance with the principle of evolution it was impossible to account for climbing plants having been developed in so many widely different groups, unless all kinds of plants possess some slight power of movement of an analogous kind. This I proved to be the case; and I was further led to a rather wide generalization, viz. that the great and important classes of movement, excited by light, the attraction of gravity, etc. are all modified forms of the fundamental movement of circummutation. It has always pleased me to exalt plants in the scale of organized beings; and I therefore felt an especial pleasure in showing how many and what admirably well-adapted movements the tip of a root possesses.

Darwin died of a heart attack at Down on 19 April 1882; he

198

Craxirex Galapagoensis: the link between the buzzard and the American carrion-feeding hawk family.

Zenaida Galapagoensis, also found on the Galapagos Islands.

was buried in Westminster Abbey on 26 April in the north aisle of the nave, a few feet from the grave of Sir Isaac Newton.

The tradition of scientific inquiry in the Darwin family, which first showed itself in the varied activities of Erasmus Darwin, was carried through into later generations, and there were few members of the family who did not possess some talent.

Charles and Emma Darwin had ten children, of whom one, a daughter, Mary Eleanor, died soon after birth and two others, Anne Elizabeth and Charles Waring, died when children. We can see from the *Expression of the Emotions* and the *Biographical Sketch of an Infant* how closely Darwin watched their development. He studied them with the same patient care which he bestowed on earthworms, beetles and climbing plants. Sometimes his sympathy affected his observation: when, for example, he was trying to record accurately the changing expression of a crying child. In later life he spoke wistfully of his children's childhoods. 'When you were very young it was my delight to play with you all, and I think with a sigh that such days can never return.' Darwin's love for his children was one of his most attractive features. Despite his daily sufferings and the highly concentrated quality of his work, he always delighted in their company and never let out a harsh word, even when they were romping about in his study and disrupting his work. His tenderness towards his children is shown by his account of his little daughter Annie who died aged ten. He spoke of her joyous spirits and her clinging, fondling nature.

When quite a baby, this showed itself in never being easy without touching her mother, when in bed with her; and quite lately she would, when poorly, fondle for any length of time one of her mother's arms. When very unwell, her mother lying down beside her, seemed to soothe her in a manner quite different from what it would have done to any of our other children. So, again, she would at almost any time spend half an hour in arranging my hair, 'making it', as she called it, 'beautiful', or in smoothing, the poor dear darling, my collar or cuffs – in short, in fondling me.

Although Darwin's health prevented him from engaging in rough pastimes with his children, he enjoyed going for walks with them and telling them stories. He helped them observe and understand the working of nature: how Drosera caught insects; the fertilization of an orchid; the relation of the sexes in thyme. An example of Darwin's mildness to his children is given by his son Francis.

200

ABOVE *New Zealand Flowers and Fruit*: Marianne North visited Australia and New Zealand partly at Darwin's suggestion.

RIGHT A painting of the Brazilian jungle by Marianne North: *Glimpse of Mr Weilhorn's House at Petropolis, Brazil.*

He came into the drawing room and found Leonard (the fourth son) dancing about on the sofa, which was forbidden, for the sake of the springs, and said, 'Oh, Lenny, Lenny, that's against all rules', and received for answer, 'Then I think you'd better get out of the room'. I do not believe he ever spoke an angry word to any of his children in his life; but I am certain that it never entered into our heads to disobey him.

Darwin's daughter Henrietta described in vivid terms his captivating fatherly qualities.

My first remembrances of my father are of the delight of his playing with us. He was passionately attached to his own children, although he was not an indiscriminate child-lover. To all of us he was the most delightful play-fellow, and the most perfect sympathiser. Indeed it is impossible adequately to describe how delightful a relation he was to his family, whether as children or in their later lives.

One of his sons, when about four years old, tried to bribe his father with sixpence to come and play with him during working hours. His children never tired of hearing stories about his schooldays at Shrewsbury and the voyage of the *Beagle*. He read them aloud Scott's novels and gave them little lectures on the steam-engine. Henrietta also wrote:

Another mark of his unbounded patience, was the way in which we were suffered to make raids into the study when we had an absolute need of sticking-plaster, string, pins, scissors, stamps, foot-rule, or hammer. I remember his patient look when he said once, 'Don't you think you could not come in again, I have been interrupted very often'. He cared for all our pursuits and interests, and lived our lives with us in a way that very few fathers do. But I am certain that none of us felt that this intimacy interfered the least with our respect or obedience. Whatever he said was absolute truth and law to us. He always put his whole mind into answering any of our questions. One trifling instance made me feel how he cared for what we cared for. He had no special taste for cats, though he admired the pretty ways of a kitten. But yet he knew and remembered the individualities of my many cats, and would talk about the habits and characteristics of the more remarkable ones years after they had died.

Another characteristic of his treatment of his children was his respect for their liberty, and for their personality. Even as quite a girl, I remember rejoicing in this sense of freedom. Our father and mother would not even wish to know what we were doing or thinking unless we wished to tell. He always made us feel that we were each of us creatures whose opinions and thoughts were valuable to him, so that whatever there was best in us came out in the sunshine of his presence.

Few children write and fewer fathers deserve so fulsome a tribute. This does not sound at all like the usual picture of the inhibited, authoritarian family life of the Victorian age. What

OPPOSITE Emma Darwin. Her marriage was a long and happy one.

205

became of Darwin's seven surviving children, after they had enjoyed the advantages of so intelligent and unclouded an upbringing? It is nice to know that his granddaughter, Gwen Raverat, was to describe the five sons (including her father) – William, George, Frank, Leonard and Horace – when all gathered together, as 'a solid block of uncles, each more adorable than the other'. Three had beards and two had whiskers and all had warm, flexible, moving voices and beautiful hands. As small boys, they probably lacked this mellow charm; when their sister Elizabeth (later Aunt Bessy) once went into the drawing-room at Down, she gave one look at her five brothers and flounced out with the words, 'Nothing but nasty, beastly boys.'

Of the two surviving Darwin daughters, Elizabeth (Bessy) never married and Henrietta (Etty) married Richard Litchfield, who worked on the legal side of the Ecclesiastical Commission. Etty had been an invalid when young and behaved like one for the rest of her life. She was more forceful and astringent than her brothers and she wrote very well about her parents and the Wedgwoods. Bessy was stout, nervous and unmarried, and kind to her nephews and nieces.

William Erasmus (1839–1914) was the eldest child and the only son who did not have a scientific kind of mind. He was, one could say, the most ordinary and least intellectual of the five brothers. He was also the most unself-conscious. During his father's funeral in Westminster Abbey, where he sat in the front seat as eldest son and chief mourner, he felt a draught on his bald head; so he balanced his black gloves on the top of his skull. William was sweet-natured, brave and simple. He had the pink cheeks, clear blue eyes and strong chin of a sailor. He looked so clean and wholesome that one of his brothers said, 'You could eat a mutton chop off William's face.' His wife was Sara Sedgwick, from one of the few important New England families, and they both lived in Southampton, where William was a partner in a bank. They lived in style and comfort in a large, ugly Victorian villa. Sara was obsessively orderly, whereas William took things very much as they came. He broke his leg trying to get through a swinging gate out hunting and had to have it amputated. After his wife's death he came to London and turned to earlier intellectual interests; he read the classics in Latin, Greek, French, German and Italian, went to concerts and picture galleries and travelled about the country, in an early motor car, looking at architecture. William stands out as the most cultured and least hypochondriacal of the brothers.

The next brother was George Howard (1845–1912) who later became a distinguished mathematician and professor of Astronomy at Cambridge. He was sent, like his other brothers except William, who went to Rugby, to Clapham Grammar School, which catered for scientific families by putting more mathematics and science into the curriculum than was normal at that time. Later he was second wrangler and then a fellow of Trinity, Cambridge.

George was surprised to find that he possessed so much mathematical ability. He had gone to London to read for the Bar, but he soon found that his health was not strong enough and he returned to Cambridge and settled in rooms in Trinity. He took his bad health as seriously as had his father; in fact, they both suffered from digestive troubles and general weakness. In other ways, also, George reminds us of his father; he had the same habit of not writing at a table, but in an armchair, and he showed the same evenness of temper when his children burst into his study when he was working. His definite entry into serious scientific life was his memoir *On the influence of geological changes on the earth's axis of rotation* (1876). Shortly after its publication he became a member of the Royal Society. Most of his later scientific life was taken up in developing certain lines of research which originated out of this memoir. He wrote papers first on the earth-moon system and later on the whole universe of stars, the object of most of these papers being to put general conjectures to the test of precise numerical calculations. He developed the theory of 'tidal friction' in his papers on the earth-moon system and thereby worked out that 54 million years ago the moon was only 6,000 miles away from the earth. Before that earth and moon had, in his view, formed a single mass and this led him to study the process by which the mass had been broken up. In Boston in 1897 he gave a course of lectures which were published the next year as *The Tides*. This little book has been praised as a masterpiece of semi-popular scientific exposition.

George's personality suggested, to the end of his life, a boyish eagerness and romanticism. He loved heraldry, history, languages and travelling. He played games with chivalrous associations – archery and real tennis; the books he read were in the romantic vein – Shakespeare's history plays, Scott and Chaucer; he liked pre-historic forts, Roman roads and mediaeval dungeons; he had a romantic feeling for places, particularly Down, and he was naïvely delighted by the many honours which he received.

Of the five brothers, Francis (Frank) (1848–1925) was the only

naturalist amongst them. As Darwin's biographer and editor, he recorded very well his father's intellectual achievements. After studying medicine at St George's Hospital, London, he turned to botany and was later his father's secretary and assistant at Down. After Darwin's death he moved to Cambridge, where he became university lecturer in botany. He helped develop a new aspect of botany, known as vegetable physiology; this was concerned with the study of the fundamental nature and mechanism of plants as living organisms. Before that the study of botany at Cambridge, and elsewhere, had been more or less restricted to the systematic definitions of plants. Frank, dashingly, had three wives. The first, the mother of the golfer Bernard Darwin, died in childbirth. The second was Ellen Croft, the mother of the poet Frances Cornford; she was tense, nervy and bohemian, smoked cigarettes and cut short her rough, black hair. The third was Florence, the widow of the great legal historian, F. W. Maitland. Frank had the usual family qualities of gentleness, humour and unambitiousness. He was an elegant writer and an accomplished musician; at Cambridge he played flute solos at the University Musical Society's concerts and he also played the bassoon, oboe, recorder and pipe-and-tabor.

The fourth brother, Leonard (Lenny), was a major in the Royal Engineers. He was not at all like a typical regular soldier and most of the jobs he did in the army were scientific rather than military: observing eclipses; photographing the transit of Venus and writing on the topography of Africa. After leaving the army on the grounds that 'his health was not very good', he became Liberal Unionist member for Lichfield, where his great-grandfather Erasmus had lived; he also became President of the Royal Geographical Society and of the Eugenics Society. Leonard was, like the others, humorous and benevolent and died aged ninety-two, having been twice a widower.

Horace (1851–1928), the youngest surviving son, spent most of his life at Cambridge. He was a designer and manufacturer of scientific instruments and he supplied the new natural science laboratories at Cambridge with their apparatus. He established the Cambridge Scientific Instrument Company. 'Go and talk to Horace Darwin' was the advice given to anyone who needed some delicate new scientific instrument. He married Ida, daughter of Lord Farrer. He and George were the two brothers who had weak health. His absorption in machines rather cut him off from other members of the family.

These were Darwin's five delightful sons. Their father once said, 'I have five sons, and I have never had to worry about any one of them, except about their health.' George's daughter, Gwen Raverat, who in her book *Period Piece* described and drew very attractively her childhood memories of the various Darwins and their households, had a feeling that her lovable uncles had never quite grown up. She emphasized this by saying that their father 'was so tolerant of their separate individualities, so broad-minded, that there was no need for his sons to break away from him, and they lived all their lives under his shadow, with the background of the happiest possible home behind them'.

At Darwin's death his loyal 'bulldog' Huxley, referring to the 'manifestation of public feeling not only in these realms, but throughout the civilized world', said that

the causes of this deep and wide outburst of emotion are not far to seek. We have lost one of these rare ministers and interpreters of Nature whose names mark epochs in the advance of natural knowledge. For, whatever be the ultimate verdict of posterity upon this or that opinion which Mr. Darwin has propounded, whatever adumbrations or anticipations of his doctrines may be found in the writings of his predecessors; the broad fact remains that, since the publication and by reason of the publication, of the *Origin of Species*, the fundamental conception and the aims of the students of living Nature have been completely changed.

What Huxley said has turned out, on the whole, to be correct. Darwin did more than any other single individual before or since to change man's attitude to the phenomena of life. He established evolution as an inescapable fact, process and concept. To that extent we are all 'Darwinists' today. What is the 'ultimate verdict of posterity' on Darwin and Darwinism? The emergence of Darwinism covered the period from 1858 to 1872; it carried all before it until the 1890s, when the anti-Darwinian reaction set in. This lasted about a quarter of a century, to be followed by a phase of neo-Darwinism which we are, so the experts tell us, enjoying today.

How has the evolution theory developed during the hundred years or more since the publication of *The Origin of Species*? Everyone now seems to be agreed that the occurrence of evolution is a fact, and biologists stopped arguing about it long ago. The neo-Darwinism theory, which is fashionable today, is still based on the Darwinian concept of natural selection as the directive force guiding the course of evolution. Although Darwin relied almost entirely on natural selection as the means of bringing about evolutionary changes in the early editions of *The Origin of Species*, in later editions he somewhat receded from this position in favour of the Lamarckian doctrine of use and disuse. He wrote that evolution had been effected chiefly through the natural selection of 'numerous successive, slight, favourable variations, aided in an important manner by the inherited effects of use and disuse of parts'. It was not long before this that Darwin had been saying 'Heaven defend me from Lamarck's nonsense.' The difference between the two theories can be illustrated by the giraffe. Lamarck explained their long necks and long front legs by their continually craning upwards to get their food; hence the inheritance of the lengthened neck and legs. According to Darwin, should there be competition for food and if there is a variation in the length of neck and legs among the giraffes, then those with the shorter necks will starve and those with the longer necks will survive. If such chance variation in the length of a neck were inherited, there would be a gradual evolution leading to today's giraffe. Many people in Darwin's day preferred the Lamarckian theory, if only because it was less repellent than the Darwinian one with its ruthless and mechanical selection of small chance variations. Later Darwinism appeared to carry the day.

At the end of the century, biologists found, to their horror, that selection did not work. Many experiments had been undertaken in plants and animals to bring out certain characteristics, and they had all failed. It began to be thought that Darwinism was a failure both in practice and in theory – and this at the very time when the intellectual world, and even the Church, were beginning to be convinced of the reality of evolution and to accept Darwinian selection as the mechanism of the process. This turned out to be a temporary eclipse and it was not long before Darwinism came back into its own.

The most important development in evolutionary theory in this century is to be found in the field of genetics. The Dutch botanist de Vries, in his book *Die Mutationstheorie* (1901) said that species were not continuously connected but appeared quite suddenly. He also re-discovered, together with two other botanists, the laws of inheritance which Mendel had propounded

Gwen Raverat's drawing of George Darwin's wife playing croquet with their children at Down House.

211

in 1865. It was thought that Mendel's laws fitted into de Vries's theory of evolution better than Darwin's. Biologists later decided that Mendel's law of 'particular inheritance' was compatible with Darwinism. Others explained satisfactorily why experiments in Darwinian selection had apparently failed; it turned out that they had been selecting from the wrong kind of variations! They should have been experimenting with inherited variations and not with those due to the environment. Today de Vries's idea that evolution occurred in big jumps, 'saltations', as Huxley had earlier called them, is thought to be wrong, and biologists believe that very small changes take place under the influence of selection, changes which are far below the obvious differences between species. The orthodox view of evolution is now Darwinism and Mendelism fused into a single doctrine.

The layman is, it must be confessed, no wiser after being told what are the fashionable contemporary theories. It is unlikely that a gifted amateur naturalist will now, or in the future, come up with a theory which will astonish the scientific world. The expensive and complicated laboratory equipment of biochemistry and biophysics manipulated by narrow-minded technicians would soon see to that. We may be almost certain that Darwin, if alive today, would not have had much influence on scientific thinking. At the time, however, he made people sit up and think about these deep and perplexing organic processes. He did this because he looked with the eyes of an amateur at subjects which caught his interest. Like Socrates and Voltaire, he asked questions which disconcerted because of their simplicity. The informality of his basic equipment was considered, even in his own day, delightfully inadequate; insects were examined on his study table with a simple dissecting microscope; he observed the habits of plants in a lean-to greenhouse at the back of his kitchen. In this, if not in the results of his work, he seemed an amateur.

What Darwin was, rather than what he did, is of interest to us today. He was, first of all, extraordinarily English, and England provided the ideal environment for his career. His interest in plants and animals began as that of a country gentleman who shot, rode to hounds and went in for beetle collecting and field botany. Then, before our eyes, occurs an astonishing transmutation – the dilettante young naturalist is transformed into the mature and formidable scientific theorizer. Try as we can to find the mechanism for this change, it will always escape us because it can be explained only by the indefinable property of greatness.

It remains today difficult to understand why this unintellectual, unambitious and uneducated man should have discovered a relatively simple theory which took by surprise many people cleverer and more learned than himself. Wordsworth described a child as 'a mighty prophet, blest, in whom those truths do rest which we labour our lives to find'. Darwin may have been such a child, unencumbered with sophisticated knowledge, with a simpler more direct approach to complicated subjects than his more learned friends Hooker, Lyell and Huxley.

It was Darwin, who took no interest in literature, politics, economics, religion or philosophy, after whom is named the Darwinian revolution – Darwin who was too lazy and too conventional to be a revolutionary. The success of his book did not go to his head – far from it. While the controversy unleashed by the *Origin* raged throughout the world, Darwin turned to the pleasant and peaceful pursuits of botanical observation.

Whether he liked it or not, Darwin's contemporaries decided that he was a revolutionary. The hard-working, amateur scientist became a reluctant revolutionary. Historians and other writers have for a long time been speaking of the pre-Darwin and post-Darwin epochs. Even those who doubt the originality of his theory, or who do not believe it to be true, admit the reality of the Darwinian revolution. It is still not clear today why a theory, which had been the subject of discussion for nearly a century, should overnight cause such national consternation. It startled both those who said there was nothing new in it and those who said that its ideas were so foolish as to be hardly worth discussing. Given the characteristics of our countrymen and knowing the kinds of scandal which they enjoy, it is not difficult to recognize several elements in the Darwinian 'controversy'. There were 'Establishment' scientists like Lyell who believed in Darwin's evolutionary arguments, but who did not wish to rock the boat by disturbing the credulity of the masses; there were the masses themselves, who asked for nothing better than to have their credulity disturbed; there were the many godfearing people who believed, we are told, in the literal truth of every word in the Old Testament; there were the polemical 'progressives' who believed with equal, although shifting, fervour in anything which sounded rational and 'scientific'. Since most people realized that Darwin's arguments were probably true, they were able to indulge their prejudices at no great risk to their 'beliefs'. What they were enjoying was the shock not of discovery, but of

213

ABOVE Charles Darwin portrayed in one of the *Vanity Fair* series of caricatures which appeared at the time of the controversy over evolution.

RIGHT *Late Autumn*: Emma Darwin was a gifted pianist and often played to her husband. The painting, in Down House, is by an unknown artist.

recognition. As Samuel Butler said, 'Buffon planted, Erasmus Darwin and Lamarck watered, but it was Mr Darwin who said "That fruit is ripe", and shook it into his lap.'

The Darwinian revolution did not have much effect on the practical work of scientists themselves. They continued with their studies much as heretofore. Darwin himself provided money for continuing and completing the *Index Kewensis*, a catalogue of flowering plants based on Bentham and Hooker's *Genera Plantarum*. The classification was that of the 'natural system' developed by French botanists of the last century to replace the 'artificial' sexual system of Linnaeus. It is amusing that this new botanical nomenclature should be in line with evolutionary theories established before the Darwinian revolution.

Darwinism was, in fact, both conservative and revolutionary. The discoveries of the seventeenth century marked, as we have seen earlier, the beginnings of the modern world, although it was not until the last century that their scientific effects began to be felt. It was then that various illustrious Victorians experienced their 'crises of faith' but the blame for them was not always laid at Darwin's door. Conventional opinion was due for a shaking and the *Origin* was privileged to be the chosen instrument for dramatizing and expressing the changes which had been quietly taking place. The implication of its theories touched upon religion, politics and society, quite apart from biology, and in this way it was a useful collective symbol for uniting various discontents.

The popular charges levelled against the *Origin* did not concern the origin of species so much as the origin of Man. Darwin certainly believed that man's physical structure was developed from an animal form by natural selection. He told Lyell, '*Our* ancestor was an animal which breathed water, had a swim bladder, a great swimming tail, an imperfect skull, and undoubtedly was a hermaphrodite. Here is a pleasant genealogy for mankind.' Darwin also believed, unlike his more idealistic friend Wallace, that the moral nature and mental faculties of man were derived by gradual modification from the lower animals. He thought he could detect most, if not all, our mental and moral qualities in particularly gifted and sensitive animals. In some he saw manifestations of intelligence which amounted to distinct acts of reasoning and in others instances of curiosity, imitation, surprise and memory. Darwin also gave examples of animal kindness pride, contempt and embarrassment; some mammals, he notice possessed the rudiments of language and of arith____ ___; cats a

216

horses certainly had imagination, as they were disturbed by dreams, and the deep love and submission of a dog to its master was getting close to a feeling for religion!

Darwin had difficulty in proving that these mental and moral faculties had been developed by natural selection. In fact, he admitted in *The Descent of Man* that he had attributed too much to the action of natural selection or the survival of the fittest. He recognized that there were also other important agents of change, such as sexual selection, the direct action of the environment and use and disuse. Sexual selection was used to emphasize certain phenomena when natural selection would have been unconvincing. The male beard had, for example, been chosen by sexual selection 'as an ornament to charm and excite the opposite sex'. Darwin also showed that speech and music belonged to the courtship pattern of our ape-like ancestors and that the 'sweeter voices' of women were developed to attract the males. To dispel any lingering doubts where he stood on the question of man's origin, Darwin stated in *The Descent of Man* that he was descended from a 'hairy, tailed quadruped, probably arboreal in its habits', and ultimately from 'an aquatic animal, provided with branchiae, with the two sexes united in the same individual, and with the most important organs of the body (such as the brain and the heart) imperfectly or not at all developed'.

Darwinism appears to mean simultaneous theorizing about religion, society, morality and politics based on the principle of natural selection. They were all subjects in which Darwin took no interest whatsoever. The term Social Darwinism is nowadays often used, to distinguish it from the specialized biological Darwinism. As Darwinism represents an amalgam of theories, it is not easy, perhaps not even worthwhile, to discuss its significance in one field of thought and action after the other. We know that many people did, and still do, find Darwinism and religion irreconcilable. The *Origin* did not raise the same outcry on the Continent as it did in England and, to a lesser extent, in America. In France, scientists found Darwin's theory superficial and unconvincing from the beginning; they disliked the notion of a mechanical principle causing the emergence of new forms from old. The educated public on the Continent were probably too sophisticated to enjoy a crude debate on religion versus evolution. Moreover, the Catholic Church took the theories of evolution more in her stride than did the different Protestant churches. Newman had himself anticipated the *Origin* and he welcomed this

217

opportunity of reinterpreting dogma to harmonize with evolution. It was not long before Catholics were told they could accept all the teachings of Darwin, including the ape-like origin of man, provided they continued to believe in the divine origin of the soul. It would be interesting to know whether the *Origin* could, or did, cause any indignation in non-Christian countries, who do not have anthropomorphic religions. Probably not; it is the terrible thought of the incarnate God, who spent some years on this planet and who took human form, being in some way related to an ape which sends shudders down the spine.

H. G. Wells describes in *The Outline of History* the horror with which religious-minded men followed the work of Darwin. He spoke of the detrimental effect of the dispute on the influential classes of the Western world.

Prevalent peoples believed that they prevailed by virtue of the struggle for existence, in which the strong and cunning got the better of the weak and confiding. And they believed further that they had to be strong, energetic, ruthless, 'practical', egotistical, because God was dead and had always, it seemed, been dead – which was going altogether further than the new knowledge justified.

Another evil result of Darwinism was 'a new scorn for the ideas of democracy that had ruled the earlier nineteenth century, and a revised admiration for the overbearing and the cruel'. Wells accused Darwinism and Kiplingism of having destroyed the dignity of government by setting up competition and survival as the basic facts of life. They encouraged, he said, brutal tribal loyalties and hatreds – of other schools, other classes, other countries. Although he regretted these particular consequences of Darwinism, he revelled as much as did Huxley in the discomfitures of formal Christianity and gloated that Darwin's theory should mean that there had been 'no first parents, no Eden, and no Fall. And if there had been no fall, then the entire historical fabric of Christianity, the story of the first sin and the reason for an atonement, upon which the current teaching based Christian emotion and morality, collapsed like a house of cards.' Since the main object of *The Outline of History* was to deny the Christian religion, no wonder that he made the most of it. Wells's book led to a minor polemical debate in the 1920s with Hilaire Belloc who accused him of ignorantly and maliciously distorting history and of not even knowing that Darwinian natural selection had been discredited long before. Belloc warned his readers against the 'old and exploded theory of Darwinian Natural Selection, upon which

OPPOSITE H. G. Wells: his account of Darwinism in *The Outline of History* was challenged by Hilaire Belloc.

218

all those popular materialists still desperately rely in their denial of a Creative God and of Design for the universe'. Belloc quoted an array of professors of botany, zoology, palaeontology and pathology from leading European universities, all of whom said that selection was unfavourable to the origin of new forms. He summed up their anti-natural selection arguments by observing that 'between the foot of the land animal and the flapper of the whale, between the powerfully defensive and aggressive great ape and the weak, more intelligent man, there must be stages (if the transition ever took place) where the organism was at a positive disadvantage, and that consideration blows Darwinian natural selection to pieces'. With those words he was satisfied that he had pricked and burst Wells' fallacious and atheistic bubble.

The name Social Darwinism has been given to every possible shade of opinion. It was used as an argument by nationalists for a strong, centralized state and by Victorian liberals for a *laissez-faire* economy. It appealed to the English sense of individuality and personal freedom and it repelled certain foreigners for the same reasons. Nietzsche said that 'over the whole of English Darwinism there hovers something of the suffocated air of overcrowded England, something of the odour of humble people in need and in straits'. Darwin would not have liked the ideological excesses released by his theories. Although he expressed himself, after a hesitant start in the *Origin*, with brutal frankness about our ape-like origins, he ended *The Descent of Man* on a cautiously idealistic note:

Man may be excused for feeling some pride at having risen, though not through his own exertions, to the very summit of the organic scale; and the fact of his having thus risen, instead of having been aboriginally placed there, may give him hope for a still higher destiny in the distant future. But we are not concerned with hopes or fears, only with the truth as far as our reason permits us to discover it.

OPPOSITE Darwin in old age – a bronze at Down House.

Further Reading

Darwin's Life and Letters, edited by his son, Francis Darwin.
More Letters, edited by Francis Darwin.
Autobiography, edited by his granddaughter, Nora Barlow.
Voyage of the Beagle, edited by Nora Barlow.
Emma Darwin, a century of family letters, edited by her daughter, H. Litchfield.
Period Piece by Gwen Raverat.
Erasmus Darwin by Desmond King-Hele.
Darwin by Gavin de Beer.
Darwin by G. Himmelfarb.
Darwin, the Fragmentary Man by Geoffrey West.
Darwin Revalued by Arthur Keith.
A Hundred Years of Evolution by Carter.
The Hookers of Kew by Mea Allen.
The Living Stream by Alister Hardy.

List of Illustrations

225

Picture research by Pat Hodgson.

The map on page 74–5 was drawn by Design Practitioners Ltd.

Index

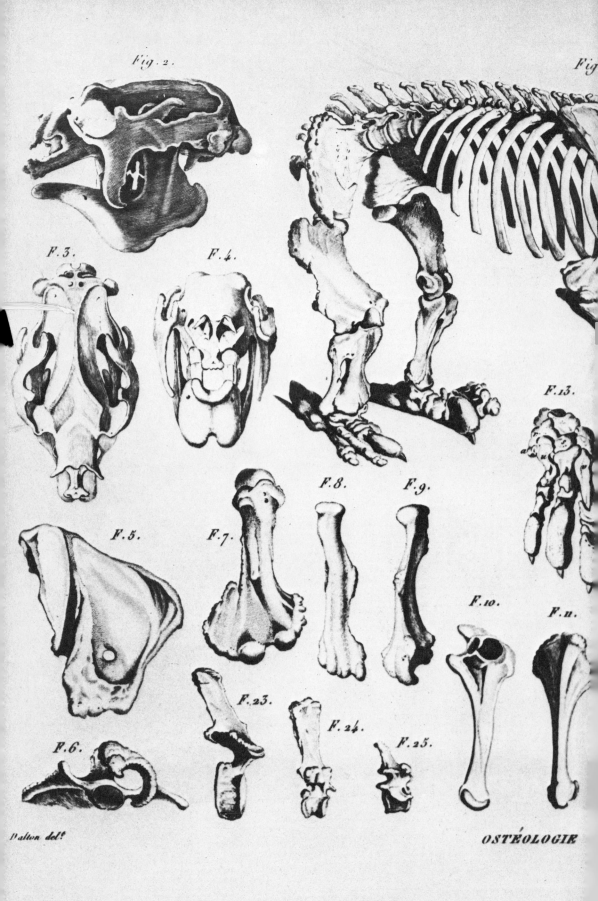

Fig. 2.

Fig.

F. 3.

F. 4.

F. 13.

F. 5.

F. 7.

F. 8.

F. 9.

F. 10.

F. 11.

F. 23.

F. 24.

F. 25.

F. 6.

Dalton del.?

OSTÉOLOGIE